· SUCCES͟

IN LETTER, WRITING ·

BUSINESS AND SOCIAL

BY
SHERWIN CODY
AUTHOR OF "THE ART OF WRITING AND SPEAKING
THE ENGLISH LANGUAGE," EDITOR OF "THE
WORLD'S BEST" SERIES, ETC.

SIXTH EDITION

CHICAGO
A. C. McCLURG & CO.
1913

897m

C 671

5

W. F. HALL PRINTING COMPANY, CHICAGO

CONTENTS

v

305432

CONTENTS

PART II

SOCIAL LETTER WRITING

PREFACE

THE days when people wrote charming long letters to their friends are past, for the newspapers nowadays tell all the news and describe the many minor happenings of the world we like to know about.

For all that, letter writing is a finer and more important art to-day than it ever was in the past. Cheap postage lays open the entire country, even the most inaccessible village, to every man, woman, or child who can write a letter. We are learning the art of shopping in New York, Chicago, and San Francisco on the same day, and important businesses are set up in New Mexico, Maine, and Alaska, whose customers may be in Florida, Hawaii, or Philadelphia.

And then in a social way, why should we be limited in the society we enjoy by the confines of a small village or a single city clique,

when we can make friends and enjoy them by
mail in the great centres of the entire world?
Why should our school advantages be limited
when we can study with the greatest teachers
in New York, London, or Paris?

The one thing to open all these gateways
is to know how to talk fluently and correctly
on paper, and make people do what one de-
sires by the words one writes. This is the fine
and delicate art of letter writing.

So far as I know there has never been printed
a book which actually tells how to deal with
human nature by mail, that really puts the student in the way to succeed in letter writing. In
fact, nothing is more certain to produce failure
than to follow the directions of the books which
profess to teach the art. They belong to an
age that is gone. There is in them no suggestion of the new art that has been making such
rapid progress during the past ten years.

The present volume is in part the outgrowth
of a somewhat unusual experience, which the
author may be pardoned for narrating.

Quite a number of years ago, while connected with a newspaper that was trying to assist its readers in an educational way, the author became aware of a wide popular demand for instruction in this art of expression for practical purposes. A series of lessons was prepared, which were tested, found useful, and finally put forth in book form.

When the books were printed they had to be sold. One day a friend offered to print a page advertisement of the books at his own expense, in a business men's magazine, and furnished the heads for the advertisement. The page was written and printed, and brought nineteen two-dollar orders the first day, and several hundred dollars' worth within a month.

One might suppose that after this it was only necessary to print the advertising and take in the dollars. No mistake could be greater. Each different magazine required a different statement. One error in statement might cost one hundred to three hundred dollars, and such errors did many times result in loss.

Circular letters were tried. One letter cost twenty-five dollars to send out and brought nothing back. Another did little better. Then one brought fifty dollars and the loss was made good. This letter was used month after month with fair profit. One day the advertiser thought of another method of statement, formulated it in a letter, and multiplied the cash returns by three.

It takes an experience like this, in which the value of every word is measured in dollars, to make one fully realize what an immense power lies in written expression.

When it became known that the author of these books had not only given forth his theory, but was making successful tests of his own powers in selling what he had written, the heads of important business houses, who were already widely successful, came to him to get help to become still more successful. Some did increase their business many thousands of dollars. The advice was formulated into a system, a series of cards, which proved their worth by helping to raise salaries and augment incomes.

PREFACE

As my "System in Business Correspondence and Advertisement Writing" was prepared for successful business men who wish to perfect themselves in the technique of dealing with human nature by mail, and so get more money for themselves or for those who employ them, so this volume has been prepared as a sort of introduction to the entire subject of letter writing, for all who wish to succeed in making people do things by the words they write on a piece of paper. Here will be found stated the fundamental elements of a great subject, the starting points, the outlook, the requirements for success. The subject is too large, the art too technical, to be taught in a few easy lessons. The boy in school may exhaust his text-books, but when he gets into the shop or the laboratory he finds that he must begin all over again from an entirely different point of view.

But this book is one that all may understand and profit by, however many or however few letters may have to be written. Numerous business men who write many letters do not even know what a power is within their reach or that a real science of letter writing exists. For such, a reading of this book should be helpful. The novice, on the other hand, suspecting that letter writing with success is not so easy as it seems, will find out what the difficulties are and how to begin to meet and overcome them.

SHERWIN CODY.

CHICAGO, May 1, 1906.

PART I

BUSINESS LETTER WRITING

SUCCESS IN LETTER WRITING

CHAPTER I

ESSENTIALS OF SUCCESS IN BUSINESS LETTER WRITING

THE growth of the mail-order business in the United States during the past five years has been enormous. Two concerns in Chicago doing an exclusive mail-order business handle over twenty-five million dollars a year each. But the important thing is that almost all mercantile houses are now trying to develop a mail-order branch. They find that they can get business by mail at less expense than they can by travelling salesmen. Even the book canvasser is giving way to the canvassing letter. One large subscription book

17

concern in New York, handling only very high-priced sets of books on the instalment plan, does its entire business by mail, without a single personal solicitor. Of course over one hundred thousand dollars a year is spent in magazine advertising; but the final success of the business depends on the skill with which the letters are written.

There are two kinds of business letters written, — mere memorandum notes, and letters which are intended to do the work of the personal visitor. These memorandum notes, such as are sent when a check is mailed, an item of information required, or an order given, would be more satisfactory if they were written on special memorandum slips instead of on letter-heads, after the manner now so generally adopted of sending orders on special order blanks. Then they would not become confused with real letters, which should be works of art to win a customer and get his business. It is of this artful letter writing that I am going to speak in this chapter.

Keeping Out of the Wastebasket

The art of getting business by mail cannot be said to be a new one, for it has been practised ever since the development of the post-office. The trouble has been that circular letters go into the wastebasket and do no good. Business men have only recently begun to find out how to keep their communications away from the wastebasket. The mechanical production of things that look like letters is only the first step in the true art of letter writing.

That letter writing is an important business is indicated by the fact that there are some three thousand business schools in the country, and at least as many more small typewriting schools, turning out from twenty-five to one thousand graduates apiece every year, a total of many thousands, each capable of writing at least ten thousand letters a year.

The marvellous fact is, however, that of all these thousands, scarcely one becomes a really efficient letter writer. The standard of American letters is preposterously low.

Poor Stenographers

A prominent business man, who has employed a great many stenographers, wrote to me the other day, "Ninety per cent of stenographers are disqualified for their work by their poor use of English. As a class they are standing still and grumbling because many of them have to work for pitifully small salaries.'' The stenographer fails because he cannot write even a correct English letter. How far, how very far is that from a successful business-getting letter!

Because stenographers are so poorly educated, and are so often devoid of mental capacity for conducting correspondence on their own responsibility, correspondents are chosen from among accountants, clerks, and salesmen. They have the business instinct, but, as a rule, know nothing of such matters as punctuation or even spelling, and leave the English of their letters and all minor details of form and correctness entirely to their stenographers.

It will therefore be seen that, while business

letter writing as a profession has immense possibilities, from the fact that so much business is now being done by mail, the profession of the business letter writer is in its infancy, — scarcely developed at all.

Big Salaries for Correspondents

To-day the big salaries in the commercial world are paid to the salesmen, who get from two thousand to ten thousand dollars a year. The salaries of correspondents at present seldom exceed the lowest of these figures; but the reason is that there are no good correspondents available to whom the business man can afford to pay more. Usually the important letter writing has to be done by the head of the house himself. Advertising men are sometimes paid high salaries, and they undertake to write important letters; but too often they do not understand the difference between a display advertisement and a personal letter. So, while the profession of advertisement writing has developed rapidly and successfully, the profession of business let-

21

ter writing is still a matter of the future. The writer believes that the time will come, and not far in the future, when the display advertisement writer will be subordinate to the business letter writer, or when advertisement writing will be but a branch of the larger profession of "publicity."

Since there is no School of Business Letter Writing which really does anything to teach the art and the profession as such, an ambitious young man or woman must educate himself or herself. We will now try to indicate how this self-education may be carried on.

Self-Education

First, letters should be correct in form. This is a matter primarily for the stenographer. Second, letters should be written in simple, effective English, which will produce the same effect on the reader as personal conversation. Third, the correspondent should become a student of human nature as revealed in letters, and should learn to write one kind of letter to one kind of person, and another kind of letter to another kind of person. Fourth, he should have a well-developed system in letter writing, so that each letter in a series will perform its own office, and the campaign as a whole will be as artfully devised as a military manœuvre. Fifth, he will master each detail by itself, and do it so thoroughly that, when he comes to dictating one hundred or two hundred letters a day, he can make every one a masterpiece, because each will be but a new combination of elements he has carefully worked out in advance.

Grammar in Business

In the first place, why need a business letter be correct? A few years ago we often heard business men say, "What do I care for the grammar of a letter, so long as it gets the business?" Now business men quite generally recognize that grammar is an important element in getting business. Grammar is the science of the logical relationship of words in sentences. If words are not put together grammatically, they

23

fail to express the meaning clearly. Bad grammar and confusion are one and the same. So, too, the man who does not punctuate his letters correctly fails to express his meaning quite completely. The impression on the mind of the reader is not quite so clear and sharp. An incorrect letter is like a slightly blurred photograph. You can tell whom the hazy photograph represents, but a picture that is startlingly clear and sharp has a vast commercial advantage over one that is not.

A few errors of punctuation and grammar in one letter do not matter much, but the same errors in a hundred letters, accumulating one on top of another, weigh vastly in the final success of a business. Successful men recognize this, and now the largest retail store in the world pays one dollar for each error in English any one of its employees finds in any of the printed matter issued by the house. Already many other business houses are following this example in one way or another. The most striking evidence in the matter is the fact that

24

stenographers who can write correct English may get twice the salaries paid to ordinary stenographers. The president of a concern in Minneapolis widely known all over the country, employing fifty stenographers, said publicly not long ago, "If all my stenographers, clerks, salesmen, etc., would learn to write correct and effective business letters, they would be worth twenty-five per cent more to me, and I should be willing to pay the full value of their services." We believe that the average stenographer could get his or her salary raised by dint of patient study of correct English during a period of six months.

What is Good Business English?

The correct English that counts is that which makes the expression clearer and sharper. Some grammarians try to impose arbitrary rules, taboo idioms,— the life of the language,— and would teach a literary style to the letter writer in place of the colloquial style absolutely required for success in business letter writing. It is well to follow the best cultivated usage, but an expression generally used by educated people is good enough for a stenographer, even if philologists do condemn it.

There has gradually grown up in commercial circles a peculiar language employed in business letters only. In every other sentence we find "beg to advise," "in regard to same," "we note," or one of a curious collection of clipped phrases from which all the small words have been omitted, as in a telegram. I call this the "commercial jargon." It is well enough understood in strictly business circles, and was not especially objectionable when business correspondence was merely an exchange of notes or memoranda between houses. Now when business men deal directly with the ordinary person in the outside world, who is familiar only with conversational English, this commercial jargon is injurious in the extreme. It gives a stiff, formal, meaningless cast to a letter, which takes away every winning quality.

A Conversational Style

I cannot repeat too often that the style in which a business letter ought to be written is that of a simple, natural conversation. The successful letter writer must have imagination, so that he can see his customer sitting before him, and in his letter can talk to that imaginary person just as a good salesman would face to face.

Then the correspondent, who talks to his customer in a letter, must be himself an expert salesman. Unless he has the innate qualities of a salesman he will not succeed as a correspondent.

However, the man who is successful as a personal salesman may fail altogether in letter writing; and a quiet man of imagination, whose figure is small or ungainly and whose manner is not prepossessing, or who lacks the glib tongue of a ready talker, may make the best possible salesman in letters. The art of talking effectively and the art of writing effectively are very different indeed. One calls for many words uttered rapidly, and much depends on the manner and personal appearance; the other calls

27

for few words artfully chosen. In the letter writer we see the embryo manager, who is more likely to get to the head of the business than the successful salesman, whose mercurial temperament has its drawbacks. So the good letter writer will be a free, effective talker on paper.

But this is not the whole of business letter writing.

Knowledge of Human Nature

Success depends on knowledge of human nature, and a tactful adaptation of the letter to the unseen customer. Plainly, the writer must have imagination, so that he can see in his mind's eye the person he is addressing,— thousands of miles away, perhaps.

It is a curious thing that letter writers get into the habit of writing letters all of a length, very nearly. A man who is a fluent letter writer will dictate long letters, and a man who prides himself on condensation will write very brief ones. The display advertisement writer especially is likely to think that the terse and epigrammatic is the only effective style.

28

The good letter writer will learn to write very short and snappy letters to those who want short and snappy letters, and long and detailed letters to those who want long and detailed letters. A few words will perhaps make a man pay out fifty cents or a dollar for something he wants, but the adventurous spirit who thinks he can get from fifteen to one hundred dollars from the average man by a short letter will find he has made a great mistake. A long, detailed, argumentative letter is required.

A farmer will usually be glad to read any long letter that comes to him, while you probably could n't get a busy business man even to glance through such a one unless he were already deeply interested. The art of interesting such a man with short letters till he is ready and eager to read long ones is part of the fine art of successful correspondence.

The personal salesman plans his campaign against a new customer with instinctive art, for, when the psychological moment arrives for a hard push he feels that it has come, and makes the push. The correspondent works more or less in the dark. Modern American letters are defective in not getting more responses from the customer, so that the letter writer may know how his canvass is progressing, and what to do. Again, the letter writer forgets what he has said in an earlier letter, neglects to write during long periods, and seldom thinks much of making one letter lead the way for another and help it to make its effect. Suppose a business man cannot be gotten to read a long letter, yet a long story is to be told him; he must be given that story in artful instalments, each short enough so that he will read it. Success in this branch of the subject depends largely on good systems and filing devices,—broad enough to cover the circumstances fully, and simple enough to be used readily and constantly. Most filing systems are so complicated and awkward that they can be used but little, and so they defeat their own purposes. System in mechanical departments is a great thing, and American business men are showing their appreciation of its value. But system in the composition of letters is just as important, — if anything, more so.

System in Letter Writing

System in composition of business letters will enable a correspondent to write one hundred letters a day and make every one of them a masterpiece. Let me try to give you some idea of how it can be done.

Let a correspondent select the class of persons he most often addresses, and an actual letter of the general type he writes most often. Let him study that letter word by word, spending hour after hour upon it. Let him write it and rewrite it in every possible way till the best way is found. Not only find one good way, but several. Take time enough to master that one letter in all its phases. Then take up another letter, of another class. Master that in the same patient way. In a few months the whole field of one's correspondence will have been worked over.

While it would be a mistake to copy a satisfactory letter, making it a mere form, certain sentences, phrases, and words may be used many times, being combined a little differently in each letter. Demosthenes did something of this sort, as did all the famous Greek orators. He had a book containing fifty or more stock perorations, or form paragraphs, which we find used repeatedly throughout even his greatest orations, though very often with suitable variations. The same general plan is admirably adapted to the requirements of business letter writing, and it is the only plan which will permit the writing of one hundred good letters a day, for so large a number of strictly original compositions is out of the question.

Specializing

Business letter writing has its different departments, each of which must be studied carefully and mastered. It is seldom that one man can handle all these departments at the same time successfully. Whenever it is possible, specialization is desirable; and it will be well for the ambitious young man to specialize. In a mail-order business, there is the display advertisement, — one type of composition; then there is the detailed follow-up letter,— another type; then there is the polite and fascinating handling of all inquiries. Often something will go wrong, and complaining customers must be dealt with in a diplomatic way so that their custom will continue,— a most important department in all mail-order business; and collections must be made, and they require a special series of letters quite unlike anything that has gone before. One may make his fortune by excelling in any one of the three departments, — soliciting letters, complaint letters, or collection letters.

I hope I have said enough to convince the ambitious young aspirant that business letter writing is not so simple as it seems. One might use with success all the talent and skill of a great and successful novelist, and still find many fields unworked. Genius and talent have full scope; but training and hard work also bring their sure reward in this as in all other fields of business.

CHAPTER II

FORMS AND CUSTOMS IN LETTER WRITING

CHAPTER II

FORMS AND CUSTOMS IN LETTER WRITING

BUSINESS letter writing has its etiquette as well as everything else. One of the first things a business man looks at when he receives a letter is the arrangement of the opening lines.

The address of the person writing should appear first, with the date. This shows the time and place of writing the letter, and unless the habit is formed of always putting this in first, the full address is liable to be overlooked altogether and the person receiving the letter will not know where to send his reply. Thousands of dollars, to say nothing of letters not containing money, go to the dead-letter office and the senders are never discovered, simply because they forget to attach their addresses.

How to Begin a Business Letter

The conventional order of the items is: (1), street number and street; (2), town; (3), county, if necessary; (4), State; (5), date. Never begin this line much to the left of the centre of the page. It is very bad taste to begin near the left-hand side of the page and sprawl the date-line clear across. Put a comma after each item as numbered above, periods after the abbreviations, and a period at the end of the line.

Then in a formal business letter the full name of the person addressed should follow, beginning flush with the left-hand margin, and his address should come in the next line, beginning half an inch to an inch from the margin. Do not let this line go much beyond the middle of the page. To sprawl an address clear across the page is considered bad taste. In modern usage it is customary to use only a short address, as the town or city and State, without street number. Two lines may be used for this address if necessary, the second starting half an inch farther to the right than the first.

38

The Correct Title

If the person addressed is a man, "Mr." should always precede the name, or "Esq." follow it. Writing "H. G. Adair," for example, without any title, is considered rude and unpolished. It is like entering a private house without taking your hat off. "Esq." is used after the name of a lawyer very frequently, and in England literary men and others who are regarded as in the class of "gentlemen," are addressed with "Esq.," while tradesmen and the like are addressed as "Mr."

If the name of a single man is followed by "& Co.," or two partners or brothers constitute the firm, "Messrs." should always be used.

If "The" is properly the first word in a company name, as "The Jones Company," "The Central Express Company," no title is required according to American usage, though in England "Messrs." would still be used, as in "Messrs. Jones Company," etc.

In Writing to Women

If the name is that of a woman, "Mrs." should be used in addressing a married woman and "Miss" (no period, because "Miss" is not an abbreviation) before the name of an unmarried woman. If it is not known whether the woman is married or single, the writer has to choose between two alternatives, the risk of making himself ridiculous by choosing the wrong title and that of seeming to be impolite by not using any title. A woman in writing to a stranger should place "Miss" or "Mrs." before her own name in parenthesis (omission of the parenthesis is considered vulgar). In the best business houses no title is used in addressing a woman if it is not known whether she is married or single. The name is written exactly as it is signed.

If several ladies are addressed together, the title "Mmes.," the abbreviation for Mesdames, is appropriate.

There is some choice as to the proper punctuation after the name and address of the party to whom you are writing. If the address ends with a State, abbreviated, the period following the abbreviation seems to be sufficient. If there is no abbreviation, either a period or nothing at all is most commonly used, but the proper punctuation is a semi-colon, it appears to the writer, and this he habitually uses. A comma is always required after the name at the end of the first line.

The next line contains the salutation, which should be written flush with the left-hand margin, not indented like a paragraph.

Capitalizing "Sir" and "Madam'

"Dear Sir" is the proper form in writing to one man, "Gentlemen" in writing to a company, and "Dear Madam" in writing to a lady whether married or single. "Dear Sirs" would be appropriate in writing to a list of individuals, and formerly it was used in addressing a company. Now it is looked on as antiquated, and it is best not to use this plural, though it is still seen occasionally and taught in some books.

41

It is the almost universal custom to capitalize "Sir" and "Madam." This is a relic of the time when all titles of address were capitalized. Now we never capitalize "sir" or "madam" in the body of a sentence, and there seems to be no good reason for doing it in a salutation. If one chooses not to use the capital, he will not be criticised.

The Salutation

The salutation should be followed by a colon, colon and dash, comma, or comma and dash. The colon and dash are the most common marks, but careful letter writers now omit the dash on the ground that it is entirely useless. In England a comma is almost universal. In this country the comma and dash seem going out of use, except in social letters. The American letter writer of the future will doubtless use the colon alone.

Careless writers frequently begin letters thus:

Mr. Smith
     Dear Sir: I received your note, etc.

This presents a very careless and vulgar appearance. The salutation should always come flush with the left-hand margin, and there should be at least two lines of the address, so that there will be an indented line between the name (flush with the margin) and the salutation (flush with the margin).

The following forms will serve to summarize what has been said about the beginning of a letter:

Alpena, Mich., Apr. 10, 19—.

Mr. J. D. Trail,
      Springfield, Ill.
Dear Sir:

---

15 Charing Cross,
London, W. C., Eng., Apr. 20, 19—.

Messrs. Jones & Brown,
      New York City, U. S. A.
Gentlemen:

700 Columbia Road, N. W.,

Washington, D. C., June 9, 19—.

The Central Express Company,

Chicago.

Gentlemen:

—————

Rae Bldg., Chicago, May 3, 19—.

Mrs. Morton Stevenson,

Portman Square, London.

Dear Madam:

—————

Appleton, McPherson Co., Wis.,

April 29, 19—.

Miss Sarah Banning,

2025 Drexel Boulevard, Chicago.

Dear Madam:

—————

The Body of a Letter

In business letter writing a liberal margin should always be left on both sides. Leaving no margin or a very small one looks stingy. Many stylish letter writers like to leave a very wide margin, amounting to half the solid portion of the letter. If the letter is long and is carried down near to the bottom of the page, this excessive margin at left and right spoils the proportions.

Paragraphs should always be indented about an inch, never less than three-quarters and never more than an inch and a half. Some people indent their paragraphs hardly at all, while others begin them quite near the right-hand margin. Both these habits are very bad form. Beginning paragraphs flush with the left-hand margin is not paragraphing at all.

There is great difference of opinion whether the first word after the salutation should be indented the same as a paragraph, or should begin just below the end of the salutation. In typewriting it is most usual simply to turn the machine up one notch and go on without moving the carriage to left or right, and this is logically the correct method. Since the salutation is followed by a colon, the paragraph may be considered to have begun with the name of the person addressed. Those who choose to begin the body of the letter as a new paragraph have ample authority, however.

It is always desirable in replying to a letter to mention the date in some way, especially if there is the slightest chance for confusion between several different letters. Letters are commonly identified by their dates.

'Avoid Stereotyped Phrases

The .stereotyped "Answering your letter of the 26th inst.," "Replying to your esteemed favor of the 19th of January," "Acknowledging your favor of the 17th ult.," etc., though long used and still commonly found, are now being abandoned by all good letter writers for an easy, incidental method of bringing in the date. It is desirable in a business letter to get at once into the subject of the letter. Begin therefore at once, saying, for instance, "We are very glad indeed to say that we have the plough described in your favor of the 19th, and shall be pleased to send it promptly on receipt of an order from you"; or "Thank you for your kind offer in your letter of the 10th, just at hand. We appreciate," etc.; or "We regret to say we cannot accept the offer made in yours of the 7th, as we have just placed an order," etc.

When no possible good purpose is served in mentioning the date, it should be omitted.

There are certain words and phrases which hitherto have been found almost exclusively in letter writing. Among them are "We beg to advise," "Referring to same," "We hand you herewith,'' etc. Good letter writers now make it a rule never to use a word or phrase in writing a letter, if possible, that would not be used in a personal conversation. The effect of a letter should be that of a short, concentrated talk, and anything that interferes with that impression is bad. A polite salutation at the beginning, and an equally polite close, take the place of the bow with which a salesman enters and leaves a private office. But no salesman would begin to announce his business in a jargon which only an experienced business man could understand. He tries to be as natural and colloquial as possible, and to make his customer feel at ease. The letter writer should do the same.

The Close

The proper complimentary close for a business letter should be either " Yours truly," "Truly yours," "Very truly yours," or, at the utmost, "Cordially yours." "Sincerely yours" should be reserved for letters of friendship. "Respectfully yours" is too formal and old-fashioned except in special letters when great deference is desired. It is not considered in good taste now in ordinary business letter writing.

The complimentary close should begin not quite half way across the page, and the first letter should always be a capital. Observe that the subsequent words never begin with capital letters. To begin other than the first word with a capital letter is looked on as a sign of ignorance.

When a letter is ended with some complimentary sentence such as, "Trusting we may hear from you shortly, we are Yours truly," no comma should appear after "are." It is indeed not at all necessary to express "we are" or "I am" in a case like this, since these words are so clearly implied, and seem to be awkwardly in the way. "With best wishes, Cordially yours," is enough of a sentence for its purpose, and so is "Thanking you for your order, Yours truly," since in both cases the verb is so clearly implied one may look on it as really there for all grammatical purposes.

Novelties in Letter Writing

Various fads may be observed from time to time, and are not objectionable when used within limits. Some people write the address at the head of a letter with every line flush with the margin, including the salutation. There is no objection to this, but the regular form is the best for daily use year in and year out.

Omitting all punctuation marks is likely to lead to confusion, and such a practice should not be indulged in.

The Envelope

The address on the envelope should be nicely proportioned, and each succeeding line begun a little farther to the right. If the address is long, one line may be placed in the lower left-hand corner, thus:

```
           Miss Sarah Hammersley,           ʼ
                   15 Woolwich Road,
                       Beverley Common,
England.                      London, W. C.
```

There is no special objection to omitting the commas at the ends of the lines, or to placing all the lines flush with the beginning of the first one. It looks very bad, however, to permit a lower line to come farther to the left than the first line, unless it is an unusually long one.

The stamp should be put always in the upper right-hand corner, for putting it elsewhere on an envelope greatly inconveniences the post-office clerks. The address of the sender should always be placed in the upper left-hand corner, so that if the letter miscarries it can be returned to the sender without going to the dead-letter office. In polite correspondence the return address is often placed on the flap at the back of the envelope.

CHAPTER III

THE PROPER STYLE IN LETTER WRITING, AND HOW TO GAIN FLUENCY

CHAPTER III

THE PROPER STYLE IN LETTER WRITING, AND HOW TO GAIN FLUENCY

THE writing of business letters is apparently a simple matter, for millions of people are writing them every day. In certain lines of business, however, highly skilled · correspondents are sought, and secured by high salaries. More skilled correspondents would be employed if they were to be found, or if business men realized how much business a poor correspondent can turn away. Business letter writing can be learned as certainly as stenography or any recognized business calling, and without doubt the strictly professional letter writer should be paid according to his ability.

First of all, a business letter should be strictly grammatical. Many business letters are not so; but even the illiterate would soon perceive the difference, and without knowing why, would prefer the business man who seemed by his letters to be master of what he professed.

The simple graces of rhetoric and a trained style would also prove useful, in spite of the limited range which business letter writing seems to have. Every letter writer often feels that he would like a freer use of words. This is nothing more or less than the ability which results from cultivating style according to the principles of practical rhetoric.

Construction of Business Letters

But full knowledge of words, grammar, and the principles of composition will not alone make a good business letter writer. This branch of composition has features peculiar to itself. The principles which govern it may be stated briefly as follows:

1. *Know the man to whom you write.* No man can write a good business letter unless he understands the person to whom he is writing from top to toe. In most cases he has never seen

this person. If he is replying to a letter before him, he can form some idea of the writer from the character of this letter, including the handwriting if the letter is written by the person who composed it. For the rest, he must judge the person from his general knowledge of the class to which he most probably belongs. In any case, the character of the person to whom the letter is sent wholly determines the form of the letter, and even what is to be said. Knowledge of the reader is the first requirement of all composition, and it would be well for the writers of fiction, and all other writers, if they realized it as the business letter writer must.

2. *Never write a longer letter than will be read.* It goes without saying that unless a letter is going to be read, it is not worth writing. Country people usually have plenty of time, and like to read long letters; busy city men and women have not the time to read long letters, and simply will not do it. It is folly to write a longer letter than the recipient will read, however important the topic or extensive the subject. If much

is to be said and it is important that each point should receive due consideration, a separate letter should be written to cover each important item.

3. *How to Condense.* All letters are necessarily severely limited in length, and the most important principle of composition for letter writers to master is condensation. This may be secured, positively and negatively, in various ways, as follows:

(a.) By *omitting* all details that the recipient of the letter may reasonably be supposed to know already.

(b.) By *suggesting* and *implying* in the choice of words and forms of the sentences as much as possible.

(c.) By stating important matters so *forcibly* that the reader will be forced (or rather induced) to think out the unspoken details for himself. This is the hardest of all to do.

Two Classes of Business Letters

There are two general classes of business letters: those which give information asked for,

58

and those intended to induce people to buy goods. Usually in replying to specific inquiries there will be an excellent opportunity to throw in a word of persuasion.

1. *Replies to Questions.* In replying to letters asking for information a full statement of all the facts is highly desirable. If a person has asked a question, he will be interested to read the reply all through. The general tendency of business men is to shorten such letters unduly. As a rule, such letters should be rather long. It is a mark of courtesy which is appreciated, and the business man never knows when his reputation for courtesy will bring him a big order, or when his reputation for crabbedness or the indifference which brevity indicates will send a highly profitable order to some other firm. Moreover, the man of sound business principles will give as much attention to small inquiries and small orders as to large ones, for there is no telling when the small buyer will become the large buyer; to say nothing of the fact that most fortunes have been made through large numbers of small sales.

59

2. *Circular Letters.* On the other hand, letters which are designed to stimulate business or secure orders, that is, which are more or less advertising circulars, are very likely to be too long, and so they are not read and only feed the wastebasket. The fault is almost universal, and it is notoriously fatal. The seller is full of his subject, full of arguments. He could talk for an hour, two hours, all day. It is therefore very hard for him to confine himself to a few words judiciously spoken.

We present two or three samples of well written letters taken from actual correspondence.

Letter from a Mail-order House. The first letter which we present was sent out by a large and very successful mail-order house in reply to an inquiry from a country man who thought of buying a buggy, and in his letter speaks of various other articles.

CHICAGO, Jan. 6, 19—.

DEAR SIR:

We have received your favor of the 4th inst., stating that you have decided to purchase our

No. 42 buggy. We wish to commend your selection. By ordering this buggy of us you will save no less than $15.00, for it cannot be duplicated elsewhere at $15.00 above our price.

We note that there are several changes you desire in it, and we are pleased to state that we can make all of these changes and the substitutions you desire without extra charge, except as follows: The price of No. 42 buggy with $\frac{1}{4}$ leather top is $42.80, according to the catalogue quotation. For leather-covered bows there will be an extra charge of $3.00; for making the dash without the nickled rail, but with a hole in each top corner as shown in No. 60 Peerless, there would be an extra charge of 50c. Dark green cushions trimmed in velour maroon-colored velvet to match the gear would be 75c extra.

We repeat the specifications:

No. 42 buggy with $\frac{1}{4}$ leather top, Armstrong single loop springs;

Piano body — 22 x 54 or 24 x 54 in.;

Bailey body loops;

Thousand-mile axles;

One-inch wheels compressed, hob style;

Rubber step pads;

Four leather-covered bows;

Leather-covered prop nuts;

Division dark green cushions trimmed in velour maroon velvet to match gear;

Gear painted maroon and striped in some suitable way;

Leather backstays;

Rubber side curtains and storm apron;

Buggy to have shafts, no tongue.

The total price for this buggy according to these specifications is $47.05, strictly net, free on board cars at Chicago.

We shall not get the buggy ready until we hear from you, because the price is a few dollars more than you thought it would be, and because you omitted to inclose any money. We do not accept orders for C. O. D. shipments unless a sufficient amount is enclosed with the order as a guarantee of transportation charges both ways, and as an evidence of good faith on the part of our customer. As we are making no exception in your case, but treat all of our customers alike, we hope you will order the buggy promptly in the regular way, and understand our position in the matter.

The shipping-weight of this buggy is about 425 lbs. and our Transportation Division will inclose with this letter information enabling you to determine what it will cost for freight laid down at your nearest receiving-point.

The word "corded" in the description of the buggy had nothing whatever to do with the bows but refers to the seams in the top lining. You know how a coat looks with corded seams; well, the lining in the top of buggy is made in this way. It makes a nicer finish.

We are glad to know that if this buggy suits you, your mother will want one also.

You are also interested in double Harpoon Hay Fork, and we would refer you to No. 5513 at 68c and No. 5517 at $1.00 each. These are fully described and quoted in our general catalogue. For wood pumps we refer you to page 100 of our catalogue.

As we are not sure that you have our latest catalogue, we are sending you under separate cover sections C and E, and hope you will be able to make selections that will be entirely satisfactory in every way. All our catalogue prices are strictly net, cash to accompany order, for goods free on board cars at Chicago, unless otherwise specified. We hope that our quotation and information on the buggy will be satisfactory, and that we may be favored with your order in due time. We promise to give the order our very best attention, and look forward with interest to your reply.

Yours truly,

JONES, SMITH & Co.

A Circular Letter. Some time ago the author received a letter in imitation typewriting, on stylish note-paper, in a stylish envelope. The imitation of typewriting was so good that few would recognize the difference between the actually typewritten address and the printed body of the letter, did not the great length of the letter suggest at once that it must be printed. The advertising manager who sent out this circular letter would never have dreamed of actually writing with the typewriter so long a letter as this, and he should have known that this fact would be apparent to any shrewd reader. The letter was addressed to a college alumnus, who in all probability would be a very busy person; so in any case it was too long to be read.

Two things should have been kept in view by the writer of this letter: *First*, the attention of the reader must be secured. This could have been done by a very short, simple letter, worded somewhat as follows: "Dear Sir: — If you wish to get the ———— Dictionary at half price and on very easy terms, you will be interested in the inclosed offer to graduates of Amherst College. The offer is so remarkable that we shall reserve a set of this dictionary, cyclopedia, and atlas combined, in your name until we can hear from you, and beg that you will do us the courtesy of replying promptly to this letter. By mailing the inclosed postal card you will receive full information by return. Very truly yours, ———.'' *Second*, it was of course desirable to have full information within easy reach in case there was the faintest glimmer of interest. Once started, the interest might grow through fostering, and perhaps it was well to present an argument on the spot; but this should have been included in a printed circular. Such a circular was inclosed; but the amount of matter given in both letter and circular was excessive. After the postal card asking for further information had been returned, the advertiser might have sent everything he had to offer.

Except for this feature, the letter was admirably written.

Some time afterwards another letter was sent, what is technically known as a "follow-up" letter. It supposed that some impression had been made by the first letter. If such was the case, an argument was in placé and a long letter was justifiable. Here is the letter, and it is a model of its kind.

A " Follow-up" Letter.

DEAR SIR:

Not having heard from you in answer to our letter making you, as an Alumnus of Amherst College, a special offer on the The ——— Dictionary and Cyclopedia and Atlas, we again address you, and as before we inclose a postal card and ask you to return it to us. We address you again for the following reasons:

First.—The enormous sale—130,000 sets—convinces us that The ——— has come to be recognized as a necessity in every home and office.

Second.— The plan of The——— is such a radical improvement on that used in other encyclopedias that it is now conceded to be a distinct advance over all other works of reference and as such is, we should think, worthy of your investigation.

Moreover, many graduates of your College have already ordered the work, and their letters testify to its wonderful value. We, therefore, now advise you that we have secured the entire edition of the 1902 issue. This contains the series of handsome colored plates, showing birds, flowers, fishes, precious stones, trees, etc., which have been included in the work for the first time. As you will see from the inclosed sample, they are printed in the same degree of mechanical excellence that characterizes every department of The ———. This work is used more than all other reference works combined, and if you like we can give you the names of people you know who own and use it, for we sell it on its merits.

We can tell you how professional men use The ———, how they find in it practical information not to be found in their text-books.

Or we can show you how the business man, limited as to his time, finds in The ——— an ever-present help, its unique system of arrangement placing all facts at his instant disposal.

Or we can demonstrate that to the man or woman whose opportunities for self-culture and advancement are meagre, The ——— is the equivalent of a working library of many hundreds of volumes.

Or we can tell you of the school child, or student, who uses The —— and thus gains an immense advantage over those who do not have access to it.

What we desire is to have you investigate our offer. This does not mean subscribing. All we want is the opportunity of explaining to you by letter what we consider the best book offer ever made.

We forward the complete set on receipt of the initial payment of $1.00, and the balance may be paid in small monthly amounts.

As we are still carrying your name on our mailing list, we inclose a card which we ask you to use in advising us if we shall cross your name off, or send you a descriptive book of The ——, containing colored plates, maps, and samples pages, with full information of our half-price offer. May we ask the prompt return of the card?

Yours very truly,

ARTHUR BROWN.

NEW YORK, Jan. 26, 19—. Per J.

An Artful Business-bringing Letter. The following letter, sent out by a New York publisher, is highly artful and skilfully worded. This, too, was a facsimile of a personal typewritten letter, filling an entire page. It is much shorter than the dictionary letter, though it is still too long. It was one in a series of similar letters judiciously calculated to rouse and retain the interest of the recipient, and that fact gave evidence that the writer of the letter appreciated the value of giving one idea at a time, in order not to overburden the reader; but he did not carry his principle quite far enough. The letter should be reduced by one-third.

NEW YORK, Feb. 4, 19—.

MESSRS. HENRY MILLS & CO.,

JOLIET, ILL.

GENTLEMEN:

As you are fully aware, the circulation of The ——— is gained by the arrangements we have perfected with hundreds of small publishers in the smaller towns throughout the United States to club the magazine with their newspaper. The —————— has been so remarkably well received by the people in these small communities and rural districts, as to make it impossible for us to fill the demands for our January and February issues, notwithstanding that we printed a quarter of a million copies of each.

In view of this great demand our edition for March and future issues until further notice will be half a million copies, and we guarantee that these copies will properly reach that number of families, the best of the mail buying class.

Let us say now and emphatically that this is not a free distribution; that the magazine is not a supplement to any newspaper; that the magazine is not circulated by department stores or other stores. It is an independent publication issued independently in each of the small towns, and is advertised, specially featured, and in other ways given wide publicity according to the progressiveness of the publisher handling it. Our method of securing circulation is merely the application of the principle that if one man can accomplish certain results, a thousand men properly directed should accomplish a thousand times as much as the first man.

Space in the March issue will cost $2.00 per line for black advertising, and $2.50 per line for color advertising. If you are looking for the most effective advertising in the mail-order line, advertising that is bringing large returns to the most particular advertisers, this is your opportunity. We specially recommend a color display for those looking for quick returns. Proofs of circulation will be furnished at any and all times; pro rata reduction in cost of advertising should our circulation not be as claimed. Can you ask for more?

Very truly yours,

THE ———— COMPANY.

This letter begins, "As you are fully aware." Of course the reader of the letter was not aware, but this is a tactful and effective way of introducing the statement that is to follow, only the writer overdoes the matter by including the word "fully." The word is unnecessary, for "As you are aware" serves every purpose; and as a matter of fact "fully" even spoils the intended effect to some extent by insisting over much, so making the reader suspicious.

The frank statement of how the circulation has been obtained is a most happy stroke. Many publishers would have concealed the facts. This one realizes that the facts are interesting in themselves to the reader and so are likely to win a hearing from him; but, also, confidence is invariably given by frankness.

The weak part of the letter is the second and third paragraphs. They insist a little too much. The reader is interested in the method of securing circulation, which will probably strike him as a clever idea. A very brief statement of the results of this scheme, selected from the most telling sentences of the third paragraph, would be appropriate. The subject-matter of the second paragraph might better have been condensed into the last paragraph, or omitted altogether. The last paragraph might easily be condensed in its wording. The tone of suggestion and recommendation is effective, since it assumes confidence and a friendly feeling; the assumption of such a feeling goes far toward producing it.

Handling a Large Correspondence

But some business man will remark, "I have to dictate over a hundred letters every day; I haven't time to consider every word in every one."

Every correspondent knows that when a hundred letters a day have to be composed, these letters are all very much alike in subject-matter; and probably the wording is very similar in letter after letter. Usually a large correspondence can be divided into a few classes of letters. Certain statements will have to be repeated over and over and over. In other letters the variations will be slight. Such a correspondence may be mastered in the following way:

Select from your copy-files letters containing the statements that have to be repeated most often, looking on them as typical letters that may be identical with hundreds of others. Study each letter, thinking of its application to as large a class of cases as possible, changing and revising the wording, reflecting on the probable reader, condensing or expanding as the case may require, until the letter is as nearly perfect as you can make it. Lay this one aside, and take up the type letter for another class, revising that in the same thoughtful, careful way. An hour or two may be spent on each letter.

In dictating, have these carefully prepared form letters at hand and shape your actual letter from the form you hold in your hand. Of course some variations will have to be made. At first you will make as few variations as possible, gradually memorizing the form letters. But as you dictate, you will think of other methods of expression, and these new methods you will introduce into the letter you have under way. By making a note of the letter, you can refer to your copy-file and extract the phrase or sentence that pleased you, placing it with your other form letters.

If this method of careful study is pursued for

several months, you will be able to dictate a hundred letters a day, and feel sure that they are all as nearly perfect as if you had spent an hour over each. You will soon memorize the forms and be able to repeat them without referring to your copies; and as you go on, new forms will suggest themselves, and you will use them, until your memory is loaded with a vast variety of special forms, any of which you can introduce on the spur of the moment, and you will possess the advantage of having given each phrase or sentence you use the most thorough and searching study. There is no reason in the nature of things why a business letter should not be the most perfect work of art that any literary production is capable of being.

Humor in Business Letters

The humorous style that is so because it is so preëminently *good-humored* would be a most powerful aid to the business letter writer if he could see how to use it. The danger always is that the serious-minded man to whom one writes

might not suspect that one were joking, and unpleasant complications might follow.

Deliberate fun is largely barred from business
letters, though it is being used more and more
in newspaper advertising. But the American
business man can fight against the deadly seri-
ousness that seems to have taken such posses-
sion of him. Letters need not be written in a
tone so fiercely earnest. Of course they should
not be flippant or frivolous, since such a tone
inevitably destroys confidence; but they may and
should be good-humored, kindly, courteous.
"Replying to your esteemed favor, which seems
to have no date," sounds like an unkind rebuke;
for what does the date matter? The mere dating
of a letter is too trifling a circumstance to be
taken in so serious a way, unless a lawsuit or
a charge of public dishonesty is to hinge upon
the exact moment at which the letter was written.

In every correspondence, too, many errors of
various kinds will arise. Those which are trifling and amusing may always be made the occasion of good-humored jest, which will usually

be appreciated, and may prove a powerful means of winning a customer. In the case of more serious errors, remember that argument, dispute, bad temper have ruined many a letter writer's career; self-control and kindly courtesy will do more to win your point than the most positive proof that you are right.

And once a business man has begun to look on "the humorous side of things," he will gradually see many opportunities for introducing the humorous style into his letters. Be very sure it will be worth a fortune to any man who can master it for business purposes.

Generosity and Courtesy. Another thing to be remembered is that all men are reflectors, and we get back very much what we send forth: if we send forth humor, good temper, and courtesy, we shall get them back; and, strange as it may seem, if we give generously, others will give to us. "Cast thy bread upon the waters, for thou shalt find it after many days" has a wonderful significance for the business man who can appreciate it. The man who makes himself cheap

78

makes a mistake, of course; but the man who frankly gives, assuming and believing that others will give to him, is usually favored as he expects and wishes to be.

Booklet Writing

In advertising-booklet writing all the resources of an accomplished literary style may be made available, according to conditions.

There are in general three kinds of booklets. The simplest is the booklet that merely describes in detail some article that is for sale, mentioning all the points in its favor: such a booklet is practically a catalogue. Or a booklet may be written to educate the customer to an appreciation of what he would gain by making use of the thing advertised. Or again, a booklet may be planned to entertain and divert, while incidentally holding the attention of the reader upon the advertised object till by unconscious mental effort he comes to think enough about the object to be curious about it, and to want to try it. This is the most difficult type of advertisement writing to accomplish with success, but it is obviously the only one that will be effective in the case of very simple objects which cannot be explained or argued about, but must be tested through the mere personal inclination of the buyer. It requires a high literary skill to produce such an inclination of the mind. It is very much like producing an inclination in the mind of the reader of a work of literature toward some moral or intellectual idea, or producing a liking for a character in a story. This suggests to the advertisement writer that he should study story-writing and creative composition.

Usually a booklet is sent to some one who replies to a short advertisement, and that fact implies that some interest has been aroused. The simplest form of booklet to meet such a demand is written in a clear, terse style. The booklet writer has the advantage over the writer of literary work in that he may be as brief as he wishes, and the more wit, information, and argument he can crowd into a few pages the better.

Sincerity, honesty, is the chief source of success. The old doctrine of P. T. Barnum that the public likes to be humbugged has been entirely exploded.

As a rule, rigid truth, if there is no hesitation or timidity in the writer, will carry conviction much more certainly than exaggeration or falsehood, even if the writer thinks he is concealing his steps perfectly. Somehow the false note always betrays itself.

The truth is, an advertisement or advertising booklet should be valuable and useful to the reader, just as a literary work should be. If it is useful, it will be kept and read; if it is not useful, it will be thrown into the wastebasket. No booklet should ever be sent out that is likely to be thrown into the wastebasket. If the subject itself cannot be made sufficiently interesting, useful information, extracts from literary works, or the like, should be introduced merely that the booklet may be kept. This is exactly the principle of the magazine or newspaper, from the advertiser's point of view: the valuable information or literary works in the periodical carry the advertising into the sight of the reader and keep it there till it has had a chance to sink into his mind, whether consciously or unconsciously. Booklet writers ought to apply the same principle and become distributors of the best there is in literature, art, and science. In this way they will not only diffuse knowledge and help to educate the world, but save millions of dollars worth of advertising literature that is now destroyed as soon as it is received.

CHAPTER IV

THE BUSINESS VALUE OF CORRECT ENGLISH

CHAPTER IV

THE BUSINESS VALUE OF CORRECT ENGLISH

A FEW years ago business men were in the habit of saying,

"What do I care for the grammar of a letter so long as it gets the business? I've been writing letters for twenty years, and I've made a fortune. I dare say you could pick my letters full of holes, but I have a sneaking idea they brought me more business than all the college professors' letters that ever were written."

Five years has seen a great change in the business world. Business men who made remarks like those just quoted have found out they are wrong. They have discovered that errors of grammar have probably cost them thousands of dollars, and they are as eager after good English as they were indifferent a while ago.

Let us see just why grammar is worth dollars to any business man.

Grammar is the science of the logical relationship of words in a sentence. If a man has a clear, logical mind, and writes with perfect clearness and accuracy, he observes all the rules of grammar whether he knows one of them by name or not. There was an idea once that grammar was a matter of authority and it was all a question of what the professors said or didn't say about something everybody understood perfectly well anyway. But this is not correct. There are a few things which nearly every one does which a man wishes to avoid so that he may not disgrace himself with the better educated classes in the community. But most errors of grammar are instances of illogical and confused statement. Perhaps the common reader can guess what you mean, but he hesitates a moment and is confused. The impression you would make on his mind is blurred. The error you have made, slight as it is, is like a hazy little cloud between you and your customer. Let this be multiplied in a thousand letters, in ten thousand, and a thousand or ten thousand little clouds have become a fog thick and blinding, which has shut out from you dollars the number of which you will never know.

We admit that there are more important things in business letter writing than grammar. You must have the goods to sell in the first place — better goods in your line than anybody else. To be successful you must have in your narrow corner of the world a trust, a monopoly — the cheapest house, or the best house, or the cheapest, quality considered, or the like.

And then you must talk to your customer in a letter just as you would in a face-to-face conversation; and if you are not a good salesman, and never were, and never can be, your letter will not get any business' even if your grammar is correct in every particular. The better salesman you are, the more money you sacrifice by poor use of words, by errors of grammar.

If you are making a fortune by using poor letters, you can make a greater one by using correct ones, and the more money you are making the more you lose by neglecting grammar.

The kind of grammar taught in schools is a mighty poor kind. It is a mass of rules, and machinery, and formalities, and stiffness, that has little of the practical value we have just been indicating. But there is a kind of simple grammar for a practical business man which is open to none of these objections. Let us briefly outline it, for it can all be stated in a few words.

Rules of grammar do not help a man to write correctly. They merely enable him to correct what he has written after it is on paper. The thing that helps him to write correctly in the first place is the habit of being careful in his expression. The first great fault to overcome is merely looseness and carelessness,— a slipshod habit characteristic of nearly all Americans.

We have defined grammar as "the logical relationship of words in a sentence." A school man warned us before we published this definition that we should regret nothing so much as this to the day we died; but we have never been so glad of anything.

There are four different relationships which a word must have in a sentence, and if it does n't have one of these it has no business there. These relationships are the parts of speech. A word may name something, and then it is a noun; or it may assert something or ask a question or express a command, and then it is a verb; or it may be placed beside another word to describe, and then it is an adjective or adverb; or it may be a connective, and then it is a preposition or conjunction. The exclamation is a little word which is a complete sentence in itself. With the subdivisions, we have seven different "parts of speech.'' Master these and you have the basis of grammar.

There are a half-dozen other things to know about the subject, and you have it complete in a nutshell. It becomes a little instrument like a foot rule which you can apply to every sentence you write and test it. Only a simple grammar like this can be used every day. The great complicated machine that is given us in school is cumbrous for the practical purpose of testing sentences all day long in business letters. It will do for laboratory tests, but that is another thing.

So you see that this little machine we speak of is a necessary tool in every business office, and like the daily balance in bookkeeping, it keeps you from losing money that might otherwise be yours if you had a proper system.

CHAPTER V

MODEL LETTERS

CHAPTER V

MODEL LETTERS

IF a letter has to be written for some special occasion it is <u>not desirable</u> to copy any set model. Every case has its own conditions and details, and while some general form may be followed, a frank, natural, colloquial statement should be made, with the certainty that it will prove to be a good letter.

Applying for a Position

A prominent Chicago business man says that he advises those who answer "blind" want advertisements offering positions to say simply, "Please grant interview." It is impossible to state your case completely in a letter, especially when you are ignorant of the character of the man to whom you write. This brief request is likely to pique his curiosity and he will make an appointment, if anything will induce him to do so.

A good letter applying for a position is one which shows that the writer knows something about the requirements of the place, and in which he speaks entirely of those qualifications in which the person offering the position will be interested. It is a mistake to state too many qualifications, for those that do not affect the position in question will only weaken the application.

A sincere, earnest, common-sense letter is the best kind to write. Here is one written by a young man just out of business college, who wants a position in the accounting department of a business house:

15 BRYDEN ST., CHICAGO, April 9, 19—.

MESSRS. HUGH CAMERON & CO.,

CHICAGO.

GENTLEMEN:

I wish to apply for a position in your accounting department.

I have just graduated from the Jones Business College, and have kept books in my father's grocery store for over a year. For two months

I had charge of a card system for Bates & Co. I am only seventeen years old, and I know my experience is limited; but I am exceedingly anxious to show what hard work and brains will do. If you give me a chance you will find me as faithful and hardworking as if I were a member of the firm, yet always willing to be taught and do any work assigned me. I care much more about a chance to learn and show what I can do, and obtain advancement in proportion to my success, than to get a large salary at once or find an easy place.

I am willing to do any kind of work you wish in the office, and if you will give me a chance I will accept whatever salary you think fair.

Respectfully yours,

Don't tell all about your own notions of what you are worth, nor brag, nor give any hint you are looking for an easy job. Most employers are more interested in their own affairs than yours, so talk about their business and keep your own personal affairs to yourself.

95

Simple Letters about Small Matters

When a simple matter is to be attended to by mail, do it in the simplest and most straightforward way possible. Never use any stiff or formal phraseology. The following is a good form to use in sending money. Always be sure to state just how much you send, in what form it is, whether bills, coin, stamps, money order, or check, and precisely what you want done with it.

Also be very careful to put in your own full address, and arrange the letter in a business-like way.

ASPEN, ARK., May 19, 19—.

MESSRS. HENRY DYER & Co.,

   115 WABASH AVE., CHICAGO.

GENTLEMEN:

     I inclose a money order in your favor for $1.54, for which I wish you to send me a copy of "Practical Journalism," price of which I believe is $1.45, and postage 9c. Prompt attention to this order will greatly oblige

Yours truly,

96

In giving an order, be sure that every necessary detail is stated so that the order can be filled intelligently.

55 Tacoma Bldg., Evanston,

July 1, 19—.

Messrs. Smith & Brown,

    Chicago.

Gentlemen:

Please send C. O. D. by Johnson's Suburban Express the following articles:

    6 cakes American Family soap;

    1 cake Sapolio;

    10 lbs. granulated sugar;

    10-lb. piece Star bacon;

    1 bu. potatoes.

I hope you can ship these goods the day this letter reaches you.

Very truly yours,

Observe that the items are separated by semicolons. The period after the last item indicates that the end of the list has been reached. It is usual to indent a list of items of this kind an inch or so.

It was formerly the practice to capitalize all important words as well as special names in lists of this kind and in bills. It is not now good usage to capitalize any but specific names of special brands or the like, leaving all common nouns with small letters.

A Hurry-up Letter

When somebody is to be made to do something as the result of a letter, especially something he does not naturally want to do, a certain literary quality must be put into the letter that will attract attention and make the person who receives the letter feel like doing what is wanted. If one is giving an order for goods, the natural eagerness of the person who receives the order to get it is usually sufficient to bring prompt action, and clearness and accuracy are the prime essentials.

But if a firm is slow in filling an order it is often desirable to write a letter that will hasten action as much as possible. Here is a good strong hurry-up letter:

55 TACOMA BLDG., Evanston,

July 10, 19—.

MESSRS. SMITH & BROWN,

CHICAGO.   .

GENTLEMEN:

Ten days ago I sent you an order for groceries, and I haven't yet received them. The order was as follows: [repeat order]

Now unless you can deliver these goods immediately, I don't want them. I have always dealt with your house, and have received uniformly prompt and courteous attention. Perhaps for some reason my former order did not reach you; but in any case, since I have waited as long as I possibly can, I am sure you will make every effort now to see that this order is filled IMMEDIATELY.

By so doing you will confer a favor upon

Yours truly,

Collection Letters

Collecting money by letter is one of the most difficult things in the world, and it requires all the art and skill possible.

99

One kind of letter will collect money from one sort of person, and another kind will do much better in getting money from another kind.

There are in general three classes of delinquent debtors. The first are those who have overlooked or neglected their obligations and need only to be reminded in the gentlest way. Such a letter as the following will usually bring money from them:

DEAR SIR:

I inclose a statement of the amount due on account of [state the account]. Could you not favor me with a check immediately, as I have heavy obligations to meet and need the money?

Thanking you in advance for your prompt attention to this matter,

Truly yours,

The second class includes those who have little money and find it difficult to make it go all the way around. In such a case evidently some one must wait, and usually you hope it will not be you.   Usually browbeating is folly.   Sympathy is the true tack.   Try to find out when money will be in hand, and get a definite promise that the indebtedness will be paid at that precise time.   Then when the day arrives be on hand with your notification, so as to be sure you are not forgotten in favor of some one more alert than yourself.   The following is a type of the sympathetic letter:

DEAR SIR:

I feel that I have been exceedingly patient in regard to your indebtedness to me of $14.65, which has now been owing for two months. I realize that you probably have many other pressing obligations, and it is a little difficult for you to care for all.   Now, however, I find it absolutely necessary to make this collection.   I do not care to use any unpleasant methods in doing it, for I have perfect confidence in your honesty of intention.   You know your resources, and you know the earliest possible date at which you can pay this account.   Tell me just exactly when

101

you can arrange payment, and if you cannot send me check immediately, I will try to wait a few days longer. But I must insist on something definite by return mail. Kindly oblige me by a prompt and frank reply.

Very truly yours,

The third class is that of the deadbeats, those who can pay but won't, and have to be clubbed into paying. For this class a brutal, threatening letter is usually necessary, but should be used only when absolutely required.

DEAR SIR:

Your account amounting to $12.97 has been due for four months now. I have sent you statements repeatedly, and written you several letters, but I have not been favored with a reply from you in any form.

I am loath to class you as a deadbeat. I should hate to believe you were a swindler. I feel, however, that an honest man would at least make a courteous reply to courteous letters. I am at a loss to know what to think in this case.

Before I sue you right in your home town, where every one will know that you have tried to get goods you didn't intend to pay for, and before I pile up court costs and fees upon you so as to double the debt already due, I write this letter to give you one more opportunity to pay up and settle the whole matter.

Unless I hear from you by next Saturday I shall order suit started. I sincerely hope you will not compel me to take that step.

Yours very truly,

Soliciting Letters

In writing a letter to sell anything, enthusiasm is the great thing. There should be no stiffness or formality of any kind; the letter should be long enough to make an impression, and the style should be that of earnest conversation. In short, the ideal soliciting letter should be one that comes as near the enthusiastic talk of a good salesman as possible, except that it must be condensed and a little more dignified than conversation needs to be.

The following is an example of the style and tone that bring business:

DEAR SIR:

This is to introduce you to the most agreeable acquaintance a man in your line can make — *a chance to get more business;* — a chance to put your proposition before the eyes and into the ears of 60,000 of the best-known buyers of business, office, and factory goods in America, a *clientèle* of the actual managers and directing heads of giant business establishments, the very men who decide the purchase of equipments and articles like yours.

You can meet and talk to these 60,000 serious, earnest, investigating, possible customers through the December issue of ———. And at a time so opportune to salesmen, so powerful, that *they will literally have to read what you say.*

Have to, because it is a part of the business duty, the very office routine of such shrewd business men to investigate every device that will in any way improve their office, their factories, their stores, themselves.

If you make any practical device of any earthly description for the office, store, or factory, here is your chance to reach the richest class of business buyers in the world,— and right during the month of all months, mind you, the cream of the year, the season of business changes, the time before New Year's, when new devices are considered and old ones thrown out, December, the harvest time of the mail-order season.

And if you make articles for the personal use and comfort of such men, remember such men have pocket-books, such men have means, such men have appetites, such men wear the best of clothes, such men — above any other class — are in a position to gratify every need, secure every luxury, buy every comfort that taste and demand may dictate.

They are the best spenders because they are the biggest earners.

You can't afford to overlook an opportunity

105

to reach 60,000 such men in the best mail-order month of the year, the commercial emperors of America, the rulers of giant industries and fat bank accounts, the custodians of overflowing cash-drawers, with expensive tastes,— every mother's son of them a possible customer of yours.

 You can't afford, we say, to miss the December ——. Get your copy in for this giant prosperous December issue, the best mail-order puller of the year. Mail it now, so as to reach us in good season before the 24th (——'s closing date), or if copy is not ready, mail us circulars and let our Advertisers' Service Bureau prepare your advertising. In any case, notify us how much space to reserve.

Very truly yours,

CHAPTER VI

FOLLOW-UP SYSTEMS

CHAPTER VI

FOLLOW-UP SYSTEMS

A "FOLLOW-UP SYSTEM" is a series of letters to be sent to a list of names of persons known to be interested in buying some article, or the like. A small advertisement is inserted in newspapers all over the country, and people write for information. The first letter sent them fully explains the thing offered, and usually is accompanied by a booklet giving still fuller information for those who seriously think of investing.

Many make the mistake of getting a good booklet and then writing a letter calling attention to the booklet. This is a grave error. The letter itself should make the first impression, for the booklet will not be likely to be read except by those who have first been impressed by the letter. The booklet serves to deepen the impression and get the order.

A letter of this kind is almost necessarily rather long. Yet it must be condensed and intense, and there is a regular order in making the psychological appeal to human nature, fuller description of which will be found in the next chapter.

Don't Send Too Much

It is a mistake to send too much printed matter with letters of this kind — the less the better, if the impression can be produced. It is of great value to know enough to stop when the impression is complete, for every word beyond that is likely to spoil the getting of an order.

If the inquirer does n't respond to the first letter, it is necessary to send a second. Many business men begin with a regret that the first letter was not heeded. This is unquestionably an error, for the person who receives such a letter is likely to be annoyed by the persistency. It is better to ignore what has gone before and try all over again to produce the impression requisite to making a sale. Sometimes fresh printed matter may be inclosed, sometimes the same booklet may be sent again. Each succeeding letter should be more intense, and usually briefer, though the printed matter may be more ample. The reason for a briefer and more intense letter is that the inquirer's first curiosity has probably been satisfied and he will be impatient of a very long second letter. Important points not made in the first should be made in the second. If the person was not in an especially expectant frame of mind when he received the first letter, and indeed was not expecting that letter, the shorter letter should come first, the longer second. About so much attention will be bestowed upon a given subject, and if that attention is largely exhausted in the first instance, there will be less left for the second; but if there was not time to exhaust in the first instance, more attention will remain for the second.

Make Every Letter Pay

Each letter should bring its own results, and if the first letter does not pay, it is certain that a second letter of the same kind will not pay. Some think that three or four letters must be written before results can be expected. This is wrong. If one good letter does n't bring business, nothing is likely to come from the second, third, or fourth. But if one letter pays well, it will often be good business to try the same list over again with a different letter to get still more business. This can be kept up often for years. But when any one letter fails to pay, either that letter is wrong, or the list has become exhausted. It requires a skilled letter writer with experience to tell which of these is the case. But even an experienced letter writer will often devise a letter that contains some error which spoils the business.

There is a custom among business men of shaping three letters which are called a "follow-up system." The first of these is usually a good letter, and the others are merely "follow-up letters." They lack the strong, intense quality necessary for success, and in many cases do not at all pay the cost of sending them out.

The best way is to write one letter that will get business, and keep a close record of results so as to be sure it does get business. Then construct another letter that will be even stronger and better than the first, and be sure that pays before sending it out widely. Then a third letter may be prepared in the same spirit and tested. If it brings results, it may be accepted and used, but if it does not it should be rejected. Each new letter should have either a new offer or a new argument or a new piece of dramatic proof. A mere reiteration of old arguments and an old offer is not as likely to be effective as something new.

Educating Dealers

There are cases when a different system is advisable. For example, suppose dealers are to be educated preparatory to sending a salesman to them: a dozen letters may then follow at intervals of a week or ten days, and each should contain a lesson in itself. Such a series of letters forms a correspondence educational course in the commodity or idea offered. Giving the points of a business offer in instalments, if there are many of them or if they are complicated, is more likely to be successful than giving the whole in one large booklet or catalogue, for example, since the receiver will give only so much attention at one time, and if that does not suffice for the mastery of the subject, another letter should be sent, summarizing the first and giving additional points. This can be carried on till the whole subject is presented, and then a strike can be made for an order.

CHAPTER VII

DEALING WITH HUMAN NATURE
BY MAIL

CHAPTER VII

DEALING WITH HUMAN NATURE BY MAIL

IN olden times every village had its shoe-maker, its miller, its furniture-maker, etc., and the genius who had some specialty that could appeal to only one or two in his town had absolutely no chance to make a business of it.

Then came the railroads, and with them the "drummers" or travelling salesmen. The miller became miller to the entire surrounding country, the furniture-maker sold his products in many cities, and a shoemaker, like a certain well-known governor of Massachusetts, became shoemaker to almost the entire country.

But there is a limit to the places to which a drummer can afford to go. All the small towns and country places aggregate as great a number of buyers as the cities, and the only cheap and practical way to reach them is by mail.

How important, then, is the art of dealing with human nature by mail!

New Mail-Order Methods

The art or science of mail-order salesmanship is so very different from that of personal salesmanship that entirely new methods are being developed, and as we all need sooner or later to know how we may use written words in letters to make people do things, all will be interested in the leading principles of this science.

In the first place, you are at a disadvantage in dealing with people by mail as compared with making personal calls in that you cannot see the effect of what is said. You work in the dark. Either the letter does it or does n't do it. If there is any hitch, you do not know it. A man may decline your offer, if he answers your letter at all, but he will not tell you why. If you are on the spot you may find out the reason why, and remedy the difficulty, but this is not the case by mail, as a general thing.

Again, the impression of a letter is far less

intense than the impression of a talk. You can talk to a man or a woman half an hour or more. No one is likely to spend more than five or ten minutes reading a letter. You must, therefore, do your business in five minutes, if at all. If you make no impression in five minutes, you probably will never make any.

Mail Solicitation not Cheap

It is a popular notion that dealing with human nature by mail is a wonderfully cheap way of doing business, if it can be done at all. A postage stamp and stationery cost but a nickel, whereas a personal visit might cost from five to twenty-five dollars. If business can be done by mail it seems as if the cost of doing it would be almost eliminated. But this is an entirely false notion.

As the impression of each letter is correspondingly less intense than that of a personal visit, so the proportion of returns is correspondingly smaller. A book canvasser may get three orders out of every five visits, whereas only one letter

119

out of twenty or a hundred will bring an order. If each letter costs five cents, and it takes a hundred letters to get an order, the cost of getting an order is five dollars.

Dealing with human nature by mail is by no means an inexpensive method, and it has its distinct drawbacks and limitations. But there are a vast number of things that can be done by mail that cannot be done in any other way. It costs no more to reach a man in Alaska than in Chicago or New York. Letters will go all over the world, and the cost of sending them varies little. It follows, therefore, that all the business that is closed to personal salesmanship by reason of distance or cost of travel is immediately opened up by the art of letter writing. Besides, whole lines of business, in which an appeal is made to scattered individuals over a wide territory, are made possible. The country is unified. Every individual may have the advantage of every other individual; and as the distribution of books and periodicals through the mail has gone far toward making culture universal, so doing business by mail will go far toward making comforts and refinements of life universal. And from the other side, every man going into business must realize that he has the world for a market.

One Letter Worth a Million Dollars

Such are the general conditions. Now let us examine some of the particular points of this art. No one who has tried to sell goods by mail will fail to realize that there is a vast difference between an ordinary memorandum letter and a good business-winning letter. One good business winning letter may be worth a million dollars, and one man may write it. In no other way can one man talk to so vast a number of people.

But if one talks to a million people, all dissimilar, it is very different from talking to one person who can be sized up and handled in a special way. The letter writer must strike an average. To do this he may have to try again and again, and he must study the effect of his letters by imagination. The salesman on the spot sees the effect with his eyes. The letter writer must see

121

the effect with his inward eye, the eye of imagination. As it takes a man of imagination to
move people through a poem or a novel, so it
takes a man of imagination to deal successfully
with people in doing business by letter.

How to Construct a Selling Letter

There is, however, a certain plan on which
a letter may be written so as to sell goods effectively. This plan has four distinct steps, as fol-
ows:

1. Create desire. Unless the demand is universal, as for wheat or coal or common clothing,
it is not safe to assume desire, and if the demand
and supply are universal, there is no profit in advertising, for the advertiser only creates a market
for some one else. But if one is selling stylish
clothing, let us say, the first thing to do is to
create a desire for style by showing how much
it is worth to the ordinary buyer. If a person
believes in style already, he is pleased to be con-
firmed in his belief, and if he has paid little attention to it, the argument is a sort of revelation

to him. We can assume only an indifferent open-mindedness, and there must be an intense desire to lead to buying. To get a sale, the first step is therefore to intensify desire.

2. Once the desire is created, the seller by letter should show just how his product meets the requirements in the best possible way. Every advertiser ought to feel that he has the best of its kind in the world, or the cheapest, or the most accessible. Success depends upon having a monopoly in one of these respects. Unless there is such a monopoly, one man's advertising only creates a market for another.

But it is not enough to say your product is the best. Every one says that; nobody believes it. But if the letter salesman shows just the points of his superiority, so that the buyer sees and understands, he is much more ready to do business. He feels he is going to a certain extent on his own sound judgment. He must be made to feel that he is exercising this judgment.

3. The third step is to offer proof. In ninety-nine cases out of a hundred one is writing to an

utter stranger, and it is important to offer some evidence of one's respectability and honesty. But even if one's reputation is widely established, the buyer wants to know if the thing in question has really been a success with others, or if the salesman merely thinks it is going to be a success.

Evidence is usually to be found in the testimony of actual users, and hence the "testimonial sheet." But conventional printed testimonials, which may have been "faked," or doctored, or obtained from friends, are of small value in comparison with facsimiles of checks, or of big orders, or detailed statements from persons who may be written to for a verification. One or two good pieces of proof are far better than a hundred ordinary ones.

4. The final step is as important as any of the preceding three, something that will clinch the order on the spot. Thousands upon thousands of dollars are wasted each year in working buyers up to the point of buying and then asking them merely to write for more information, instead of asking them to give some sort of order,

or in some way committing themselves to an order.

Moreover, the first step to be taken should be as easy as it is possible to make it. If the person must go to the postoffice for a money order, the time required will let him cool off and change his mind. If he may merely reinclose the letter he has received with a dollar bill, and put them together into an addressed return envelope, the effort required is reduced to a minimum, and the maximum of orders may be anticipated. Also, while the buyer takes the important step he must be made to feel that he can retrace it at any time. Human nature seldom does retrace its steps, but it always wants to feel that it can. The great mail-order firms now make it an almost universal practice to advertise very prominently that if the buyer is not satisfied in any way, or even changes his mind, his money will be refunded without a question. The percentage of refunds is very small if the advertising is at all genuine, and the risk of sending money through the mails unregistered is very slight as compared with the loss of business that would result if it were considered necessary, as it once was, to require a money order, registered letter, or draft.

Trust Human Nature

On the average, human nature is honest, and if one avoids writing to known tricksters (the average agent, for example, from whom full pay in advance should always be required), there is little danger of loss, even though the opportunities for stealing and trickery seem enormous. And the small loss that may come is to be charged off as one of the necessary and fixed expenses, just as bad accounts are in all merchandizing.

Different Letters for Different Classes

Success in dealing with human nature by mail depends to a considerable extent on appealing to classes, studying each class as in personal salesmanship one would study each individual, and making the class appeal as personal as possible. By this method one may write a letter going to ten thousand, and yet it will read as if written exclusively for each person who receives it.

The broadest classification is that of sex. You must write to a woman in a very different way from that you would use in writing to a man. You may argue with a man; you must show a woman. She wants a picture she can look at, a sample she can feel, a descriptive explanation more emotional than argumentative. The quality' of the stationery, the excellence of the printing (sometimes the poor quality is more effective than good would be), and the whole feeling and atmosphere of the proposal are usually more important than the arguments. Indeed, in writing to a woman it is well to suppress argument, or simplify it down to the point required in writing to a child. The spirit, the enthusiasm, are the most important things.

There are also the people who have time to read long letters, and those who will look at nothing that is not reasonably short. Mail-order houses dealing with farmers find that they like long letters, even on unimportant topics, and all letters to them must have a certain length.

Women usually have plenty of time, and if interested, will read a long letter, which a busy business man would throw in the waste basket.

Business men, who receive large amounts of mail, demand that a letter shall look peculiar, shall be out of the ordinary, and not too long. Yet the letter must be long enough to do the business in hand. Nothing irritates a business man so much as a letter so short that it tells only half the story. There has been an idea widely prevalent that all letters must be as brief as possible. Successful mail-order business men are finding out that a selling letter must have a certain length in order to get business, even from the busiest person in the world. In selling real estate a letter of two or three solid typewritten pages is required to handle the business. Yet, if a letter of three lines will serve the purpose (as if one were to offer a keg of emery at carload price), that is the right length for a business man, though a woman or a farmer would require a letter ten times as long.

People Buy as They Feel

People buy or refuse to buy largely as they feel, rather than as judgment dictates. There must, therefore, be the greatest care to avoid rousing prejudices except in one's favor. A word that carries an objectionable atmosphere, a statement that suggests even a personal criticism or injures vanity, ·may undo the best argument. Tact in letter writing is even more important than in personal salesmanship, for if a mistake is made it is made forever and cannot be corrected or overcome.

It is clear that something approaching the highest and finest literary art is required in doing business by mail. The writer of a book which rouses men to action, or the orator who sways and influences his audience, are doing much the same that the letter writer undertakes, namely, using words so as to make people do things. The chief difference is that the business letter writer is only trying to sell, while the writer or the orator usually appeals to higher motives. The work of the novelist and the orator may unquestionably be of a much higher order, but probably the mere technical skill required is less. The novelist and the orator, swayed by genius, know not why they succeed. The letter writer must depend on cold-blooded craftsmanship.

Literature and Letter Writing

The man of eloquence and literature writes or speaks expansively, stopping only when he and his audience are tired. With the letter writer condensation is the great secret of success. He can never take the chance of tiring his readers. In a few hundred words he must create desire, demonstrate his mechanism, or the merits of his product, prove his case, and get his order. The secret of this wonderful condensation is selection and intensity. Only telling items must be chosen, yet they must seem to be all there are of importance, or the impression must be given that all the rest are just the same.

A letter which can bring dollars day after day to a business house (or a magazine advertisement for that matter), especially when the money comes from people of education and intelligence, must be a work of fine art. Days, weeks, months, may have gone to the production of it. Sentence by sentence, word by word, it has been discussed and studied from every point of view. Then it is tried and the results are carefully measured. In the case of no other kind of writing is the test more severe or more direct, or the opportunity for conscious skill more obvious. In doing business by mail there is opportunity for the highest talent; yet prolonged training is required. No one supposes that the art of business letter writing is God-given, as many suppose the case to be with literature. Yet no one will deny that ability of a high order is indispensable.

As the possibilities latent in merchandizing by mail develop more and more, it will be seen that the opportunities within the reach of one man will be simply enormous, as one letter or one

advertisement may reach millions, and the proportion of business that will result from the right
letter or the right advertisement will be so much
greater, that an enormous fortune may lie in the
difference between a common letter and a really
good one.

PART II

SOCIAL LETTER WRITING

PART II

SOCIAL LETTER WRITING

CHAPTER I

FORMS AND CUSTOMS IN SOCIAL
CORRESPONDENCE

UNRULED paper and jet black ink are imperatively required. Ruled paper is for the use only of children who have not learned to write straight. Colored or pale ink is bad form.

Cream white paper is always right, but pale blue and gray are frequently used. No other colors are recognized.

For social correspondence the paper should be thick, and in double sheets, either note or billet size. The double sheet used for social correspondence is to be folded but once, in the middle, from side to side, and the envelope should be square, or so as to fit the paper when thus folded. If the paper is square, the envelope will necessarily be oblong.

Crests and monograms are falling somewhat into disuse, and in their place we now find the house number and street, usually without the city or town and State, about three-quarters of an inch from the top of the sheet, in the middle, or a little to the right of the middle. Black, red, blue, or brown may be used for the lettering. A monogram and the address together are sometimes used. Men often include the name as well as the full address, placing them in the left-hand corner.

Abbreviations and Figures

In social correspondence the abbreviations and figures common in business correspondence are not permitted.

Figures are to be used only for the house number, and in informal notes for the day of the month, and hours.

Only titles of persons are abbreviated, but

"Reverend" should not be abbreviated, and should be preceded by "the."

Days of the month, days of the week, and the months, should be spelled out in full in formal letters written by women. The year is usually not given in social letters.

Arrangement of a Social Letter

If the address is engraved at the head of the letter, the date may be written first, just below the address, a little to the right, as "January the tenth," "Tuesday the tenth," or the like; or the date may be placed at the end, after the signature, on the left-hand side, and if the address is to be written it also may be placed at the end before the date. It is usual to place the date at the head in the case of long letters, and at the end in the case of notes.

In social letters it is very unusual to give the full name and address of the person written to, either at the beginning or the end of the letter, if the salutation includes the name. In very formal letters beginning "Dear Sir" or "Dear

Madam," the name and address or name alone should be written at the beginning, on the left-hand side.

In social letter writing the margin required on business letters is not insisted on, because the size of the paper is so small that all the space possible is needed for the writing. Care should be taken not to crowd the letter, however.

Typewriting is not permitted in social correspondence.

The Salutation

In writing to a person with whom one has no social acquaintance the formal "Dear Sir" or "Dear Madam" may follow the full name, as:

Mr. HENRY ARTHUR JONES,

    DEAR SIR:

or

Mrs. JAMES H. ANDERSON,

    DEAR MADAM:

The address after the name may be omitted only in strictly social letters. If the letter is one on business, the regular business style is to be adhered to, though ladies are permitted to employ social forms in business letters.

Official letters begin "Sir" or "Madam," omitting the "Dear."

All ordinary social letters begin "My dear Mrs. Blakely," or "Dear Mrs. Blakely." "My dear" is considered more formal than "Dear" alone. After "My," "dear" should never begin with a capital.

If the name is contained in the salutation, it should not be written above.

"Dear Friend" or "Friend Jones," and similar salutations, are no longer considered good form.

The proper punctuation after the salutation is a colon or a comma and a dash. The comma and dash are perhaps most frequently used by ladies, but men accustomed to writing business letters seem to prefer the colon.

The Close

The most commonplace close for a social letter is "Very truly yours." The plain "Yours truly" is not considered good form in a social letter. "Very truly" and similar forms which omit "yours" are not looked on with favor.

A lady will usually sign herself "Cordially yours," or to a more or less intimate friend "Sincerely yours," and a man "Faithfully yours," or "Sincerely yours," or "Yours very sincerely," or the like. "Respectfully yours," "Your obedient servant," etc., are no longer in fashion.

The close should always harmonize with the salutation. To begin a letter "My darling Marie" and sign it "Yours truly" or even "Cordially yours" would be an absurdity.

Observe that only the first word of the complimentary close should begin with a capital letter, and this close should not be placed too far to the right or the left of the paper.

A lady usually signs her own full name. If she is unknown to the person she addresses she may add below, usually to the left, and in parenthesis, her husband's name preceded by "Mrs.," as "(Mrs. Henry James)"; or she may precede her own name by "Mrs." or "Miss" in parenthesis. For a woman to sign herself "Mrs. Jones," or "Mrs. Luella Jones," or the like, with no parenthesis about the "Mrs." is considered especially vulgar. Some ladies with social pretensions do this when writing to a servant or tradesperson, to avoid the familiarity implied in signing their names. Such letters should be written in the third person, however, or with the "Mrs." in parenthesis.

A man should sign either his initials or his full name. Women very seldom sign initials. If a man uses his middle name and indicates his first name with an initial, it is better to drop the first initial altogether. A middle initial is permitted. This, however, is largely a matter of personal preference.

It is considered bad form for a man to attach any titles to his signature, either before or after, and such a signature as "Dr. Brown" is distinctly bad form.

Notes in the Third Person

A lady in society, instead of writing ordinary business letters, addresses servants, tradespeople, etc., in the third person. In letters of this kind the name of the person writing always comes first, and is immediately followed by the name of the person written to, as "Mrs. Henry Brown would like to have Mrs. Maguire call Tuesday evening to see her in regard to washing some laces. It will be considered a favor if Mrs. Maguire will be punctual at eight o'clock."

Of course *me*, *I*, *you*, *us*, etc., indeed all pronouns of the first or second person, should never be found in a note of this kind. Under no circumstances should the name of the writer be signed at the end. It always appears first.

This form sounds like an affectation if used in addressing servants or tradespeople with whom the lady is well acquainted. A person who has suddenly come into social position will sometimes adopt this method, but the lady of natural breeding will write to subordinates almost as she would to social equals, though carefully drawing the line between friendliness and familiarity. It is friendliness to subordinates that binds them to one's service, and a quiet dignity and indescribable reserve effectually keep them in their places.

Invitations

There are two kinds of invitations, the formal and the informal. For the informal, friendly notes are usually written; for the formal, engraved cards or note-paper sheets are common, though the same style is followed if the invitations are written by hand.

There is no better general form. than that used by the English ambassador at Rome, who has engraved blank cards in which the name is filled in by hand. The date may also be left blank to be filled in in the same way.

Sir Augustus and Lady Paget
request the pleasure of
.... 's company
on Thursday evening, November fifteenth, at
ten o'clock.
The favor of an answer is requested.

R. s. v. p. (for *Répondez, s'il vous plait*) —
notice that only the first letter should be capitalized — seems to be giving way to the plain English "The favor of an answer is requested."
One of these forms is used only when it is important to know whether the person invited is to
come or not, as in the case of a dinner party,
luncheon, theatre party, or the like, for which
provision has to be made in advance. Many
omit this even in such cases, on the ground that
every well-bred person will have the innate courtesy to accept or decline immediately all invitations to dinners, luncheons, etc. Invitations to
"at homes," general receptions, large church
weddings, and the like, require no acceptance

or declination except the presence of the person at the time indicated, or cards sent at the time of the function or soon after.

It is well to include the house number in invitations, as in the following:

> *Mr. and Mrs. Joseph Duryea*
> *request the pleasure of*
> *Mr. and Mrs. Henry Somerset's company at dinner*
> *May second, at seven o'clock,*
> *4465 West Fifty-ninth Street.*

Invitations to receptions, teas, balls, dancing parties of any kind, etc., when sent out by a lady are usually in the form of ordinary " at home " cards:

> *Mrs. Henry James*
> *Miss James*
> *AT HOME*
> *Wednesday, November fifth*
> *at ten o'clock*

Dancing   *547 Tenth Street.*

In place of "Dancing" may appear "Garden Party" or whatever the function may be.

A gentleman, however, is never "at home," but in issuing invitations must always "request the pleasure of ————'s company" or "the honor of ————'s company."

Clubs in sending out invitations use a somewhat different form, such as —

The honor of your presence
is requested at the New Year's Eve Ball
of the Lake Shore Yacht Club,
on Tuesday evening, December Thirty-first,
at half-past ten o'clock
1919–1920.

No name is inserted, but the various members send these invitations with their personal cards, and usually admission tickets are also inclosed, which are taken up at the door by the attendants.

The word "ball" may not be used in any private invitation, though it is commonly

146

found in invitations to public or club enter-
tainments.

Acceptances and Declinations

Invitations are accepted or declined in the
same form in which they are sent, and should be
addressed to the persons in whose names the
invitations are issued. Thus:

Mr. and Mrs. James Fielding
accept with pleasure the polite invitation of
Mr. and Mrs. John Barton for dinner
on January fifth,
at seven o'clock.

The date, etc., are always repeated.

As the acceptance is usually written on an
ordinary sheet of note-paper, it is usually best
not to try to adjust the lines as they are in an
engraved invitation, but to write simply —

In place of "Dancing" may appear
Party" or whatever the function may be.

A gentleman, however, is never "at home,"
but in issuing invitations must always "request"
the pleasure of ———'s company," or "the
honor of ———'s company."

Clubs in sending out invitations use a somewhat different form, such as—

*The honor of your presence
is requested at the New Year's Eve Ball
of the Lake Shore ... ... thirty-first,
on Tuesday evening, ...
at half-...*

No name...
bers send...
cards...
inc...

found in invitations to public or club[?]
tainments.

Acceptances and Declinations

Invitations are accepted or declined [in the]
same form in which they are sent, and sho[uld be]
addressed to the persons in whose nam[e the]
invitations are issued. Thus:

Mr. and Mrs. James Fielding

accept with pleas[ure] [the po]lite invitati[on]

Mr. and M[rs.] [of] [Mr. and Mrs.] on for dinne[r]

[f]ifth.

clock.

[a]lways repeated.

The [invitation] is usually w[ritten]
[on] [n]ote-paper, it
[acros]t the lines
[on], but to r[ight]

21 Waverly Place,

January third.

Mr. and Mrs. James Brown accept with pleasure Mrs. Henry Field's polite invitation for dinner on Thursday evening, January seventeenth, at seven o'clock.

Regrets may be worded as follows:

21 Waverly Place,

January third.

Mr. and Mrs. James Brown regret that they are unable to accept Mrs. Henry Field's polite invitation for dinner on Thursday evening, January seventeenth, on account of a previous engagement.

January the first

My dear Mr. Browning:

Will you give us the pleasure of your company at dinner on Wednesday evening, the eleventh, at seven o'clock? We expect Mr. and Mrs. Gordon, whom I believe you know.

Very sincerely yours,
Helen M. Blakely

January Second

My dear Mrs. Blakely:

I heartily appreciate the honor you do me by your invitation to dine with you on Wednesday, the eleventh, at seven o'clock, and I accept with pleasant anticipations of an unusually delightful evening.

Faithfully yours,

J. R. Browning

Envelopes

A married woman is addressed by her husband's name preceded by "Mrs." When there are several daughters in the family, the eldest daughter is addressed as simply "Miss Worthington" or the like, and the others by their names, as "Miss Luella Worthington." If there is danger that the letter may go astray, the full name of the lady in the first instance also should be written.

Though a married woman signs her own name, it is not considered good form to use it in addressing an envelope to her, as "Mrs. Grace H. Cummings," but rather use her husband's name, even if he has long been dead, as "Mrs. S. H. Richardson," though when a woman is in business she is usually addressed by her own name.

In addressing business letters to persons or firms residing or doing business in the same city in which the letter is posted, either the name of the city follows the street address (or, if there is none, the name) or its place is filled by the word

" City." In the case of social letters the same rule is followed, with the preference more often given to " City," perhaps.

A comma after each item except the last, which is to be followed by a period, is the usual form of punctuation, but nowadays many omit all punctuation marks except to indicate abbreviations and set off titles, as in " James Cooke, Esq."

Postal Cards

Postal cards are usually avoided in social correspondence, and all terms of affection or endearment are omitted, including usually the ordinary salutations and complimentary closes. They are used almost entirely for sending a word of greeting when one is on a journey and nothing else is available.

CHAPTER II

HOW TO BE AGREEABLE IN A SOCIAL LETTER

HOW TO BE AGREEABLE IN A SOCIAL LETTER

THERE is as much difference between a brilliant social letter writer and an ordinary dull one as there is between a brilliant conversationalist and a stupid one. The art of written expression, however, is so different that many a good talker makes a very poor letter writer. Yet a good letter is one that comes as near as possible to producing the effect of a good talk.

Suppose you have met a young lady you like, and as you sit down of an evening you think of her and her lively ways and wish you could go across the street and make a call upon her. But she is far away, and the best you can do is to write her a letter. You place yourself at your desk with pen in hand, and immediately all the gay things you would say to her if you were calling upon her, evaporate, and you begin to make some stupid, commonplace remarks, and realize that your letter is not going to be a success.

The reason for your failure is that you lack imagination, and if you wish to succeed you must cultivate imagination. If you can see the young lady sitting opposite you, and can hear her lively replies, you will proceed to keep up your end of the imaginary dialogue and produce a brilliant letter. But if your imagination is incapable of filling in all the blanks, and you can only respond to her lively sallies (which you do not hear), you will be as dull as if you were writing to a fencepost.

But what shall you talk about? you ask.

When two people meet they talk about themselves, their likes, their dislikes, their friends, the parties they have been to, the plays they have seen, the books they have read. These are the best subjects for friendly letters, if the letters are to be more than mere notes (which are not letters at all).

All depends, however, on the character of the person to whom you are writing, just as your conversation would be very different if you were talking to a gay young girl, or to an elderly spinster, or to a sedate married woman.

If you are writing to a young lady who has shown a liking for you, and whose society you have enjoyed, probably the most interesting thing you can talk about to begin with is yourself. Let us try the experiment:

MY DEAR MISS BRADLEY:

I have just come into my bachelor den after dinner, and as I sit alone smoking my pipe my mind has wandered over the list of my acquaintances to pick out the one with whom best of all I should like a quiet little chat. I have decided that if all my women friends were across the street, and I could find any one of them "at home" on whom I should choose to call, I would select you without a moment's hesitation. I am in just the mood when I need the tonic of your gay remarks, and when I should be completely happy if I could hear your sweet music — the gentle touch of your fingers on the piano or the sympathetic sweetness of your voice.

.   .   .   .

That would do for the young lady who had a sentimental turn; but for the married woman who had condescended to like and entertain you, a very different vein would be required for success. Such a woman would be insulted by the familiar sentiment that would just please the girl.

For example:

MY DEAR MRS. BRADLEY:

Here I am in New York, comfortably settled in my bachelor quarters, but without a single woman friend within reach who can correct my morals and solace my loneliness. If you were here, I know you would take pity on me; but since you are not, let me spend an imaginary evening with you.

Let me describe my den. It is two blocks east of Fifth Avenue on Forty-fourth Street. I have three rooms, and one of them is — will you believe it? — a kitchen. I am very proud of my cooking. I can broil a beefsteak to a turn, and make as good a cup of coffee as — not as you, no, but much better than our cook used to make at home.

Of course I get my luncheons down town, and I go every night to dinner at Madame Chichina's. Her *table d'hôte* Italian dinners at forty cents beat anything I ever tasted in any other public eating-house, I don't care at what price. I never know what is coming, I always eat up everything set before me, and however hungry I am, at the end of an hour I am always satisfied. I never saw anything like it before. And it agrees with my digestion so perfectly that I regard it as better than any medicine.

But it takes an hour. You can't get served with all the courses sooner. Then how I wish I had opposite me to talk to some of the old friends at home! How we would discuss Bernard Shaw's latest play (I saw it the other night, and Loraine in the title part was great), or the latest novel, or the picture shows, or the New York social atmosphere, or how a young man should behave toward unmarried girls — when he can't get within a block of one in this self-contained city.

.   .   .   .

Social letter writing is distinctly a literary art. There are two elements that are essential; the first, to have thoughts in which your friend will be interested, or which you can share with that friend, and the second is the gift of expression by written words.

No man or woman can be a successful social letter writer unless he has the gift of friendship, the sympathetic heart that loves and the intelligence to understand the friend who is loved. Social letter writing must be more or less personal. If the personalities of the friends do not serve as a subject to write about, still the subject must be their common likes and dislikes, their common thoughts about books and affairs and men and women. You cannot entertain your friend unless you know the nature of your friend, and what will appeal to him or her. It is hard to write a good social letter to a perfect stranger, since there is nothing in common of which you know, and which you can write about.

But the gift of friendship and sympathetic knowledge of your friend are not the only requirements. Expression in written words is an art in itself, and one absolutely essential to success in social letter writing. How is that all to be learned?

The best way to learn it is to rewrite good models. Find some letters such as you yourself would like to write, written by the best letter writers, and write letters of your own, about subjects with which you are acquainted and in which your friends will be interested, but just as nearly like the models as possible.

One of the best models for modern letter writing is Stevenson. Two volumes of his letters have been published, and any man or woman who will rewrite all those letters, one after the other, at suitable intervals, can hardly escape being a pretty good letter writer so far as the art of written expression is concerned.

Another good book of models for the modern letter writer is the small collection of letters to Gladstone's daughters which Ruskin wrote. They are simple social friendly letters such as any man might write to young women acquaintances, and they are full of the charm and grace of the most accomplished of modern writers of English.

Among old writers, Charles Lamb is perhaps the best. His letters, published in several editions, are among the most charming of his compositions. He had the gift of friendship highly developed, and he had the gift of literary expression also. Of course his letters are a little antique in style. In rewriting them it is necessary constantly to try to find modern phrases for those Lamb used which are no longer current; but this effort at translation will be one of the best exercises for the more or less advanced student.

These three writers are probably the most accomplished and the best to imitate of any within the reach of the modern student, and these three are enough. It is better to master a few than to range over many without carefully studying them.

If a model of a hard, commonsense, practical style is desired, Franklin is the best writer to study and imitate; but very few will care to sacrifice grace and charm in letter writing.

CHAPTER III

HOW TO DECLINE WITHOUT OFFENCE

CHAPTER III

HOW TO DECLINE WITHOUT OFFENCE

NOT the least difficult or essential phase of letter writing is the art of apology in a letter, of declining without offence, of saying disagreeable things in an agreeable way.

There is probably nothing so brutal, nothing so cutting, nothing so disappointing, that it cannot be said in such a way as to bind a friend rather than drive him or her away.

The secret of the whole art is sympathetic consideration for the feelings of the person written to. Excuses may be hollow, apologies may be empty, but they save friendship. On the contrary the most agreeable thing in the world said in an abrupt way may ruin friendship.

The art and habit of apology can be learned. Indeed abruptness is often a bad habit into which a person falls without thought, and does not signify the unkindness that seems to dwell in it.

But at bottom the keeping of friends is a matter of unselfishness. The person who thinks all the time wholly of himself or herself will not be likely to be polite in letter writing, but the person who thinks habitually of the feelings and disappointments of others, will inevitably be polite and give no offence.

It is all in the point of view from which a letter is written. The person who thinks, "I won't do it. I know you won't like it, but I can't help it," will be sure to write a letter that will drive away all friendship. If, on the other hand, the thought is all of the disappointment that will result to the friend, of the unhappiness that this suffering will cause the person who is forced to decline or deny, the denial itself is almost lost sight of, and is passed with very little notice. It is a universal rule that if attention is fixed on one thing (such as the apology, the disappointment the refusal will cost), a person will be oblivious to the actual refusal.

Let us take so simple a matter as refusing a loan to an impecunious friend. Perhaps you have adopted the rule that a loan is not to be made to a friend unless you are in a position to consider it a gift. The friend has some pet project he wishes to promote; he feels sure he will win and be able to repay you twice over, but you suspect from experience that he will be unfortunate, and it is better for him not to make the venture at all. Now, if you think only of your desire to keep your money, and tell your friend you can't afford to waste your means on his wildcat ventures, you will offend him. If, on the other hand, you concentrate attention on your regret, he will be led to think more of your friendship than of your refusal, and while he may be irritated for the moment, he cannot be permanently offended. Such a letter as this might answer the purpose:

MY DEAR CHARLIE:

I certainly wish I were a millionaire, for if I were it would give me the greatest pleasure in the world to make the loan you ask. I am driven to refuse because my funds are so very limited I cannot do what you wish just now without great personal inconvenience. You will not think my friendship the less, however, and sometime when your need is greater, perhaps my resources will be more ample.

However, I wish I might console you. Just think of it in this way: Destiny has already fixed the fact that you would lose or win in this adventure. If it has been decreed that you lose, my inability to help you will prevent your being under an unpleasant obligation to me, you will be saved the worry of squeezing yourself to pay off a debt you can ill afford; and if you are no happier by reason of the good fortune that might possibly be in store for you, you escape the unhappiness involved in failure.

I know consolation of this kind is not very satisfactory, but you, I am sure, will take the will for the deed, and believe me still your friend, only waiting for an opportunity when fate will permit me to serve you better than I can on this occasion.

With best wishes, as ever

Sincerely yours,

A letter like this is good-tempered and friendly, and it is difficult to quarrel when there is no one to quarrel with. If you felt contempt toward your friend for asking the loan, it would be sure to creep into your letter, and he would feel angry at the injustice of your contempt. If you do not permit yourself to feel contemptuous or disagreeable, there will be little reason for your friend to feel so. His feelings will be very much what yours are. This is a world of reflections. Fill the air with blueness, and blueness will come back to you; fill it with yellow sunshine, and yellow sunshine will be reflected back to you.

Let us take a different situation. You are a lady, and a friend of the same sex has invited you to a theatre party she is very anxious to have you attend. Some more agreeable opportunity opens before you, and you do not wish to accept the first invitation. Since your reason is a selfish one, you will probably act in a selfish way and give the offence that a selfish person would give. A man in such a situation would send curt regrets; a woman would probably do nothing at all. Both would give lasting offence. In either case a polite and friendly letter would save any lasting ill-feelings.

Such a letter should not contain any lies. It is easy enough to give false reasons, which will satisfy for the time being but give still greater offence when they are found out. The true art is to tell the simple truth (or so much of it as you choose) in an agreeable way; and this is a genuine literary art. The following letter might answer:

MY DEAR MRS. BRADLEY:

I am afraid you will hardly forgive me, but I am going to tell you that it will be impossible for me to join your theatre party Wednesday evening. You don't know how sorry I am for the chance that makes this impossible. A thing for which I have been working for a long, long time has developed in just such a way that I must sacrifice either my pleasure or my interest, and I know perfectly well which you would advise me to do. If I could tell you all the circumstances I am sure you would say I could not do otherwise than forego the great pleasure you have planned for me. I appreciate your kindness and thoughtfulness in my behalf none the less. I am just as grateful to you, and I hope some time in the future to more than make up for the present unfortunate combination of events.

Find some one else to take my place better than I could fill it myself, and may you have the most delightful time in the world!

With much regret, as ever,

Most sincerely yours,
Evelyn Brown.

The thoughtfulness involved in making the effort to write a considerate letter like this does much to atone for the disappointment of the refusal.

CHAPTER IV

HOW TO MAKE AND KEEP
FRIENDS

CHAPTER IV

HOW TO MAKE AND KEEP FRIENDS

LETTER writing as a fine art resolves itself into the art of being able to make and keep friends. The great letter writers are the persons like Stevenson and Ruskin and Lamb, who had a real talent for friendship, while men and women otherwise great who have lacked this special talent have failed as letter writers. It is the art of friendship that develops the art of friendly expression.

The world is full of lonely and isolated people who long for friendship, but fail to find it. The reason for their failure is lack of systematic effort to get it. A certain timidity may interfere with personal conversation and social pleasures; but letter writing is always a resource left to these timid ones. If the pleasure of brilliant conversation is denied one, a certain cleverness of expression in letters may often be cultivated in place of it and go far to compensate the loss so deeply regretted.

In all literary expression, the human nature involved is of far greater importance than the form. Yet we find books filled with forms, and few in which any hint is given of the fundamental human conditions.

Suppose, therefore, that you have resolved to cultivate friendships by letter. With the usual natural human selfishness you probably set your eyes with longing upon those more brilliant and entertaining than you are yourself, and you feel disappointed if you do not win their attention at once.

The mistake is your own. Success in anything seldom comes from ambitious striving for what is above you, but rather from effort to serve that which is below you, not in a spirit of charity, but of broad human sympathy.

There is always in the world some one just a bit more lonely than you are who would appreciate your attention. Even from a literary point of view you can do far better in a letter to such a person than you can to one just above you. When you have to raise your eyes ever so little you acknowledge yourself the subject, another your superior and master. When you lower your eyes in the slightest degree, you become the superior, you are master of the situation. Your timidity gives place to firmness, you express yourself freely and effectively, and the success you feel in your efforts engenders a still higher success. In literary expression, success is one of the most important generators of success.

Choose, therefore, for your correspondents those whom you believe will appreciate your letters, those to whom you can write with a certain feeling of freedom. Some you will find responsive. Your success will stimulate them to an equal effort, and their response, which is the sign of your success, will in turn stimulate you. The thing that is needed on your part is patient, systematic effort.

The secret of success in social letter writing is gracious attention to those who will appreciate your courtesy. That systematic courtesy on your part begets courtesy in others, and you are surprised to find how much courtesy there is in the world — for like a sun you shine with courtesy, and it is reflected back to you with additions and variations.

But permanent success in making and holding friends by letter requires something more. Courtesy is the manner. It is a kindly robe the writer throws over all his words, a sunshiny atmosphere, a graceful carriage.

The manner is certainly of great importance, but the matter is of greater. Of what subjects shall friends write to each other to make friendship deeper?

The literary form that seems most nearly universal in its appeal is the novel. It is the expression of sentiment and the emotional problems of life. The subject of letter writing between friends who wish to make letters a means of cementing friendship should be sentiment, love, religion, ambition, happiness. There are two permanent characters, the writer and the reader

180

of the letter, and everything that is written must be of equal interest to both. The most interesting topic to your friend is your friend himself or herself, and the most available source of illustration of what you know is yourself. So the first topic to write about is your friend, and, of course, all the outside matters that come to your attention bearing on this subject. It must be an impersonal discussion, since personality might give offence. And yet the effect and bearing will be intensely personal.

What you know of an emotional or personal nature which you can say that will be of interest, you must have learned from your own emotional experiences. Your experiences are the source of your knowledge. So for success in this kind of writing you must have been an observer of yourself. Many have never formed the habit of self-observation, and so they never have anything to say that is worth while.

But it is of emotions that are past that you can write with most success. Telling all one's private affairs, entirely without thought of their interest to the reader of the letter, is very likely to result in boredom and disaster to the correspondence. The personal has pitfalls on two sides, the side of offence and the side of boredom. The true art consists in personality clothed in the garments of impersonality, always designed for the entertainment of the person who reads, and not for the relief of the person who writes.

There is a very close connection between story writing and personal letter writing. The two arts are much alike, and the successful story writer is likely first to have been the successful personal letter writer. The letter art is narrower and easier, and there are few who cannot practise it with success, while story writing should be reserved for genius.

The proper treatment of personality, sentiment, and emotion in friendly letter writing may find the best possible model in literary fiction. To read the novels of the day, or see the current plays, and talk about them, is one of the best foundations for the good letter that can be

imagined. The expression in the book or play
will be wider, more technical, more varied, but
it will be in highly developed form very much
what good writing in the personal letter should
be. There ought to be in the letter some nar-
rative of things that have happened, such as
your visit to the theatre or your buying or bor-
rowing of the book, some description such as
a picture of what you have seen or read, and
some dialogue, such as would be required by
the introduction of an occasional anecdote. And
nothing is more fascinating than the application
to your own life or thought or condition of the
principle illustrated in the work of imagination.
The novel or play you must think of as written
especially for you and the illumination of your
problems which may result; but it is your part
to select, consider, and apply. This you can do
to best advantage in a letter. A letter about a
book or play has a double advantage, in entertaining your friend, and forcing you yourself to
analyze and apply what you have seen or read.
The works of literary art form a bond of union

between the whole world, but in this union you should do your part, and that part is most obviously the discussion of literary works in conversation and social letters with friends who will respond in their turn.

CHAPTER V

HOW MEN SHOULD WRITE TO WOMEN FRIENDS

CHAPTER V

HOW MEN SHOULD WRITE TO WOMEN FRIENDS

ONE of the most delightful forms of social intercourse is the writing of letters to friends of the other sex. One is judged quite as much by one's skill in doing it as by one's behavior in a lady's parlor, but it is delightfully more personal, intimate, and suggestive. It is rather like the social *tête-à-tête*, the confidential chat in the boudoir. Men and women seldom take the trouble to write very much to acquaintances of the same sex unless they find them congenial, indeed genuine friends. In such a friendship lie many of the deepest pleasures of life, and nothing is more refining, educating, and stimulating.

All success in social relationships lies in restraint, in perfect personal control. If a man has the elements of this control in his nature, there cannot be the slightest danger or impropriety in corresponding with any lady, married or unmarried, young or old. If this element of restraint is developed, there is hardly a subject on which a well-bred, well-educated man may not speak even freely to any equally well-bred and well-educated woman.

There are certain bounds and limitations established by conventionality which must be observed, however. Unless he can count himself an intimate personal friend, no man has a right to send a woman a letter oftener than once in two weeks. The postman notices how often he leaves a letter in a given handwriting; other members of the family notice, and if a given man writes oftener than once in two weeks his letters become an embarrassment for the lady who receives them. If their relation of intimate friendship is well known to all members of the family, and especially if other members of the family may share in the letters, it is permissible to write as often as once a week. But only lovers write oftener than this. Many husbands and wives when separated write daily, but even this is laughed at by outsiders.

Again, letters must not be too thick. Bulky letters are quite as likely to embarrass a lady as too frequent letters. Two double sheets of note-paper is considered the limit. If one would write much one must cultivate the art of a miniature caligraphy. That one writes a sprawly hand is no excuse for writing a bulky letter.

Again, no gentleman will write to a lady on the typewriter, least of all, address the envelope with the typewriter, unless he is very intimate and is requested to use a typewriter so that (because of his poor handwriting) his letters may be read. The general supposition is that a type-written letter is dictated to a stenographer, and as one would not hire a young woman to go along and do one's talking for one, so it is not considered respectful to intrude a mere employee into one's social correspondence. Only business letters are to be written on the typewriter.

Some men are very fond of calling women by their given names, and writing to them as

"Dear Alice" or "Dear Jessie." When there are many sisters in a family and "Dear Miss Alice" is the only alternative to "Dear Alice," it is usually desirable to drop the "Miss" as soon as growing acquaintance will permit it without offence. In such cases it is always safe and wise frankly to ask the lady whether she will permit the liberty. When an unmarried lady is generally known among her friends by her surname, it is to be presumed that she does not care to be addressed by her given name, and he would be a man wanting in the instincts of politeness who would change "Dear Miss Gardner" into "Dear Alice." In the case of a married woman anything but "Dear Mrs. Blank" would be an extreme rudeness except in the rarest cases, almost the only excuse being the habit of having used the given name before marriage. If one had been writing to a lady as "Dear Jessie," it would seem offensive and unfriendly to change suddenly upon her marriage to "Dear Mrs. Winkley." But those who did not know the lady before marriage should never follow the example of those who did, and address her by her first name.

I have spoken somewhat at length of this etiquette of the letters a man may write to a woman, because they do not come up in personal intercourse as a rule, and many a man is puzzled when he "takes pen in hand."

A word may also be said on the close of the letter. It is usual to sign one's full name. Initials are a trifle more friendly. The given name only should never be signed unless the lady is in the habit of addressing the writer by that name. "Cordially yours" is condescending. "Sincerely yours" is the best form to express true friendship. "Yours" seems hasty and ambiguous, since it may mean much or nothing. "Affectionately" is very proper between brothers and sisters, and may even be stretched to cousins, but is dangerous between mere social acquaintances. "Dear friend" suggests the countryman, but in itself is not a bad way of beginning, and "Your friend" is the proper close for that beginning.

As I have said, "restraint and consideration for others is the characteristic of a gentleman." It is especially easy to become too intense in writing to women, and then all the delight and charm and pleasure are spoiled.

The ideal style in writing to women is one that is light, humorous, and courteous. Write precisely as you would talk to the lady in her drawing-room, only better if possible. There is usually no more fascinating subject than yourself and herself, your pleasures and her pleasures, the books you read and the books she reads, the plays you see and the plays she sees, and last but not least, the friends you have in common. Success in letter writing consists almost precisely in writing as a good talker would talk. Stiff, literary English is out of place in a letter. At the same time a certain degree of slang and looseness of expression may be tolerated in conversation that would be very offensive in letters. Letter writing differs from conversation only in this slight degree of restraint and systematic care for correctness in grammar and punctuation.

The best training for social letter writing is much reading and talking about books. Unless a man reads much and talks about the books he reads, he is very unlikely to be a successful social letter writer. The familiar language of novels is not far removed from the correctly conversational style for letters; but the most perfect models are the letters of men like Lamb and Stevenson.

CHAPTER VI

MEN'S LOVE LETTERS, THEIR POSSI-
BILITIES AND LIMITATIONS

CHAPTER VI

MEN'S LOVE LETTERS, THEIR POSSIBILITIES AND LIMITATIONS

WE know a certain bookstore which sells eight thousand books on writing love letters each year, three thousand on writing business letters, twenty-five hundred on correct English, etc. Evidently writing love letters is the most nearly universal form of literary art. Very few escape the necessity some time in their lives for writing at least one series of letters of a more intensely personal kind than any others that are ever written.

What ought a good love letter to be?

To answer in a word, it should be an intensified form of all that goes to make a good letter of friendship.

If the writer is a man, he addresses a person of the opposite sex who presumably has a finer and more delicate sympathy with him than any one else in the world, a person drawn to him by mystic ties of personal affection which cannot be analyzed ·nor understood, a person he hopes will be his life companion, soul of his soul, flesh of his flesh. And as he sits down to write there appears before him a beautiful vision, the soft outlines of a figure hallowed by love, or the striking, audacious beauty of a rebel who is adored. He takes up his pen and the crowding thoughts and emotions drive all power of expression from his mind. He thinks, he feels, he loves, but words fail to depict his passion.

The first thing is restraint. Until the emotion is mastered, it cannot be expressed; and if it is desired to win the woman, self-mastery is most certainly the thing that will do it. A woman will very seldom trust herself to an entirely abandoned lover. He must give promise of the power of self-control.

And what first of all shall a man talk about? Why, what else but the woman herself! The great mistake that men make is to talk of themselves, of their passion, their desire, their devotion. That is the last thing to talk about. That is the mistake we all make in our letter writing — we talk of ourselves rather than of and for the person to whom we write. Few women will not read with pleasure what another says of them, and it is only when the writer comes to the boring topic of himself that the letter goes into the wastebasket.

And what shall a man say of the woman he loves? Perhaps she is to him a vision too mysterious to make it possible for him to talk rationally about her. The easy way to begin is with describing the vision. Then there are all the happy days of the past to recall and dwell on, all the deep problems of life and love to discuss and apply in a personal way, all the future to picture and build up in glorious dreams. The lover may reveal his inmost emotions, he may talk of anything that is delicate and beautiful and true, he may reveal secrets that no one else has ever heard. But he must do it thinking always of the pleasure or the pain that will be caused in the heart of the reader. His selection of the things that will give pleasure, his suppression of the things that will give pain, will show the measure of his really unselfish devotion. A passion that can only pour out abuse and reproach is sure to be selfish, and is seldom rewarded by a final happy outcome.

Books on letter writing are usually consulted by the timid, and among these no doubt will be some who will wish to know how to reveal the tender emotion,—in other words, how to propose.

The only good way we know is to sit down and write a dozen or two of letters saying all that can be said, and end by sending some brief and simple announcement, such as "Margaret, I love you. Will you marry me?" The writer has never yet met the woman whose curiosity and interest would not be piqued by so brief and simple a letter as that.

However, the great thing is to avoid elegancies and stiffness, such as are usually given in books on love-letter writing, and say in the simplest possible language what it is in the heart to say.

We can hardly imagine a worse form than one like this:

MISS OBERLY:

I write to beg the humble privilege of laying my heart and hand at your feet. My heart is burnt up with love for you, and I feel that I can never be happy unless you condescend to vouchsafe to me some sign of your regard. I make bold to ask you to become my wife, and to accept the poor life-service which I can give you. Will you not tell me soon whether I have anything to hope for.

Affectionately yours,

All such forms as these seem stiff and unnatural when compared with the simple, direct, natural expression of one real heart talking to another real heart. Each case has an individuality of its own which requires a letter peculiarly its own.

CHAPTER VII

WOMEN'S LOVE LETTERS

CHAPTER VII

WOMEN'S LOVE LETTERS

MOST of the advice that men give to women on matters pertaining to feminine etiquette and propriety has seemed to us slightly ridiculous, or at any rate very crude. There are women who give advice to their own sex, and it seems to come gracefully enough from them; but if a man is to instruct women it should be by some more indirect and subtle method than plain advice.

The writer can, however, tell what kind of letters from women please him best as a man. From this point of view a man can certainly speak with more authority than any woman, and perhaps, looking at the matter from this point of view, a man is better qualified to say what is wanted than any one else.

We like the graceful, courteous, kind little notes that women alone seem to know how to write. They do not say much, the woman never seems to "give herself away," but their grace, their liveliness, and their kindness always win one.

While women seem to like to have their given names fondled, so to speak, in a letter, we think men as a rule do not care so much for this, and the woman who continues to write "Dear Mr. Oberly" instead of "Dear Frank" long after she has become "Dear Margaret," loses nothing in a man's estimation. The thing in a letter that pleases a man most, however, which is like a kiss upon the lips at meeting, is the signing of a woman's given or pet name. This is the last test that a woman may use to find out whether she really is loved or not, for the man who fails to respond to this sign of affection will probably never respond to anything.

There is a fiction that the man does all the wooing and the woman is only negatively responsive. In a majority of cases, however, it is the woman who does the active courting, only she cannot use the direct, crude methods that are proper for a man. She may not say "I love you, will you marry me?" but a sudden rosy flush in the cheeks on some auspicious occasion may proclaim the feeling and ask the question quite as effectively. She may not whisper "honeyed nothings" in the ear of her lover the third or fourth time she meets him, but she may linger with him at the door, or detain him in the hallway longer than is precisely necessary, and the effect is identically the same. She may not allow herself to press his hand until he has acknowledged his love, but the result is the same if she lets her hand rest in his a second or two when she might have withdrawn it.

In letter writing the same subtle arts are open to a woman, and a man values her in proportion as she understands and uses them. A woman may not write an ardent letter to a man she knows but slightly, but it is quite within her province to ask him to lend her a book and then send a dainty little note of thanks, filled with her pleasure at his thoughtfulness. Some may condemn this as hypocrisy, but it is a kind of hypocrisy that men thoroughly enjoy. When dainty little notes begin to arrive at a man's house, he quickly understands what they mean quite as much as the woman understands his thick and clumsy letters. Let both beware not to send too many.

When a certain point of intimacy has been reached with a man, many woman tell their love quite as frankly and straightforwardly as men do themselves; but men seldom care for frankness of this kind from a woman, even in response to their own frantic appeals. All beauty is more alluring when seen through a gauzy veil, and the woman who veils her emotions, however thinly, is always much more effective than she who exposes her soul in crude nudity.

Suppose, for example, a situation arises in which a frank discussion of personal relations seems imperatively demanded, The barbaric way is to state it bluntly; the refined way is to present it as a case in a novel, the situation of a friend, or the like. The true lover will quickly see the meaning, and the man who fails to see it is better let alone or given over as a hopeless case.

But when once a woman is engaged to a man she really loves, then comes the opportunity for the fullest and frankest self-revelation and tender expression. What she says is as if whispered to her own soul; and as her confidence in her lover grows, she will be able to say more and more, and there will be no danger that it will be misunderstood.

A few years ago a book appeared entitled "An English Woman's Love Letters," purporting to be the actual letters of a real woman. It afterward developed that the book was written by a man, and many of the critics ridiculed it; but the writer always felt that they were the kind of letters a woman would have written, and judging as a man, knows of no better letters to serve as models here. The following is the first letter in the series:

"*Beloved*, — This is the first letter from me, yet it is not the first I have written you. There are letters to you lying at Love's dead-letter office in this same writing — so many my memory has lost count of them!

" This is my confession: I told you I had one to make, and you laughed: you did not know how serious it was for me to be in love with you long before you were in love with me, — nothing can be more serious than that!

" You deny that I was: yet I know when you first really loved me. All at once, one day something about me came upon you as a surprise: and how, except on the road to love, can there be surprises? And in the surprise came love. You did not *know* me before. Before then, it was only the other nine entanglements which take hold of the male heart and occupy it till the tenth is ready to make one knot of them all.

" In the letter written that day I said, 'You love me.' I could never have said it before; though I had written twelve letters of my love for you, I had not once been able to write of your love for me. Was not *that* serious?

"Now I have confessed! I thought to discover myself all blushes, but my face is cool: you have kissed all my blushes away! Can I ever be ashamed in your eyes now, or grow rosy because of anything you think or I think? So! — you have robbed me of one of my charms: I am brazen. Can you love me still?

"You love me, you love me; you are wonderful! we are both wonderful, you and I.

"Well, it is good for you to know that I have waited and wished, long before the thing came true. But to see *you* waiting and wishing when the thing *was* true all the time — oh! that was the trial! How not suddenly to throw my arms around your neck and cry, 'Look, see! O blind mouth, why are you famished?'

"And you never knew? Dearest, I love you for it. You never knew! I believe a man, when he finds he has won, thinks he has taken the city by assault: he does not guess how to the insiders it has been a weary siege, with flags of surrender fluttering themselves to rags from every wall and window! No: in love it is the women who are the strategists; and they have at last to fall into the ambush they know of with a good grace.

"You must let me praise myself a little for the past, since I can never praise myself again. You must do that for me now! There is not a battle left for me to win. You and peace hold me so much a prisoner, have so caught me from my own way of living, that I seem to hear a pin drop twenty years ahead of me: it seems an event! Dearest, a thousand times, I would not have it otherwise: I am only too willing to drop out of existence altogether, and find myself in your arms instead. Giving you my love, I can so easily give you my life. Ah, my dear, I am yours so utterly, so gladly! Will you ever find it out, you, who took so long to discover anything?"

If I were to recommend a book of model love letters to those desirous of finding the best models, I would suggest the love letters of Robert and Elizabeth Barrett Browning. Few of us will have the power of literary expression which they had; but if we are to make any progress we must choose models considerably beyond us.

CHAPTER VIII

MODEL LETTERS OF FRIENDSHIP

CHAPTER VIII

MODEL LETTERS OF FRIENDSHIP

CHAPTER VIII

MODEL LETTERS OF FRIENDSHIP

NOT long ago there appeared a small volume of Ruskin's "Letters to M. G. and H. G.," which have seemed to me the highest models of charm in social letter writing. I cannot better conclude this book than by quoting three or four of these letters:

ARTHUR SEVERN's, HERNE HILL, S. E.,
WEDNESDAY, 24TH JULY, 1878.

My dear M——,

Please send me just a little line, and tell me what time dinner is to-morrow.

Of course that 's only an excuse to get a little note, and be able to tell F—— that I 've got one, because I could as easily ask at the door; but you may as well have my London address in case you have any orders for me. The doctors say I never obey orders, and, of course, I never do any of theirs. But there are some orders I am too obedient to, for the peace of my old age!

Ever gratefully and affectionately yours,

J. RUSKIN.

Of course the names in this letter were written in full, not as initials. And it is to be remembered that this was sent from an old man to a young woman to whom he wished to pay graceful little compliments,— none other than the daughter of Gladstone.

NATIONAL GALLERY,
FRIDAY, 28TH JULY, 1878.

My dear M——,

You were a perfect little Mother to me last night. I didn't feel safe a moment except when I was close to you. Look here, I've got notice from George Richmond and Acland saying they're both going to try to find me this afternoon. And I should like to see them, and have that music to hope for all

218

this evening and to-morrow morning; and, besides, I want you to give me a cup of tea this afternoon at five, and if you can't, you can't, and never mind; but I'll just ask at the door, and it's of no consequence, as Mr. Toots says. You can't *tell* me you can't, *till* I ask at the door; because I don't know where I shall be. And I'll come for my music at three, to-morrow, instead, and you needn't say I may, because I must and will.

And I'm ever your devoted,

J. RUSKIN.

What prettier letter of apology than the following:

BRANTWOOD, CONISTON, LANCASHIRE,
SUNDAY, 30TH SEPTEMBER, 1878.

My dear M——,

How dreadfully I've behaved to you; it's *not all* F——'s fault, but partly her ponies' fault, who bewildered me by standing on their hind legs, or going eighteen miles an hour; and partly the dogs' fault, who are

always getting between *my* legs, or pulling my
hair, or licking my face; and partly her place's
fault, which is really too pretty and too good for
her or anybody else, and drove me half crazy again
because I couldn't paint it up and down and both
sides everywhere; and partly her people's fault,
who wanted to "show" me things, and wouldn't
understand that it was a vain show, and that my
heart was disquieted within me; and partly my
own fault. (I meant to have said "of course,"·
but shouldn't have meant it.) And so I did n't
answer your letter; and now here's your forgiving — *partly* forgiving, at least — but laconic
note, and, of course, I deserve it — them, I mean,
— both the forgiveness and the Laconianism.

Well, yes, I can come on the 9th, or on the
10th, or on any day you want me, pretty nearly.
("You" is to have an emphasis, mind, but I've
underlined too many words already.) But what
does the Duke of A—— want to see me for?
He used to be so grim, at the Metaphysical,
I never ventured within the table's length of
him. But look here — you know (emphasis on

"you" again) that, though I shall mightily like studying woodcraft with Papa — Papa wouldn't have got me to Hawarden all by himself, and Mr. G——, you know, wouldn't have got me to Dunira all by himself — and I should very much like to meet the Duke, of course, yes — but . . . Please do you know if M. C. 's coming too?

You see I can come on the 10th, but after this time of utter do-nothingness at Dunira, I really want to see a little bit of and about books (they're all standing on their hind legs at present, and the printer's rabid). And I meant, really and truly, to have written this morning to say I was at Mr. Gladstone's orders from the 25th on; but now I'll do just what you tell me will be exemplary, and what I ought to do, and that is, come whenever you please, not *before* the 10th. But, quite seriously, I cannot *stay* more than two or three days at utmost, for I am indeed not well, and the excitement of conversation breaks me or bends me, banefully always. This was so even before my illness, and you know if

Mrs. W—— had not forced me, I never should have ventured to Hawarden, and you must be a dear good little Mother to me, and take care of me every minute all the while I am there. Love to Papa, though, and very true and respectful regards to Mrs. Gladstone, and I 'm ever,

Your obedient and affectionate,

J. RUSKIN.

AMIENS,

28TH OCTOBER, 1880.

My darling little Madonna,

You are really *gratia plena* (don't be shocked, I am writing about the Saints all day, just now, and don't know when I 'm talking quite properly to my pets), but it is unspeakably sweet of your Father and you to forgive me so soon, and I'm inclined to believe anything you 'll tell me of him, after that; only, you know, I 'm a great believer in goodness, and fancy there are many people who ought to be canonized who never are; so that — be a man ever so good — I 'm not idolatrous of him. If it's a Madonna, it's another thing, you know, but I never for an instant meant any comparison or likeness between D. and your Father—they merely had to be named as they were questioned of. On the other hand, I know nothing about D. whatsoever, but have a lurking tenderness about him because my own father had a liking for him, and was in great grief about my first political letter—twenty (or thirty?) years ago—which was a fierce attack upon him.

I do trust nothing more will ever cause you to have doubt or pain. I can't get what I have to say said; I'm tired to-day—have found out things very wonderful, and had—with your letter at last—more pleasure than I can bear without breaking down.

Dear love to your father.

Ever your grateful,

St. C.*

* St. Chrysostom — St. John the Golden-mouthed — was a nickname given Mr. Ruskin by Mrs. Cowper Temple.

These are the graceful little notes that women write so well and men enjoy so much. But men can write them too, as Ruskin demonstrates.

THE END

9 781022 666405